Probate and Letters of Administration Made Easy

Vivien Osarenmwinda Ekomwerenren

2019

Probate and Letters of Administration Made Easy

Published by:
A. E. Ogbeide-Ihama & Co.
Publishers of *Law Reports of Courts of Nigeria (LRCN) and other titles*
23A, Agbonmoba Street,
Between 2nd & 3rd East Circular Roads,
Benin City, Edo State,
Nigeria. (08035407994)

ISBN: 978-978-973-047-6

Printed in Nigeria by:

Chikatex Prints
2, Oghogho Street,
Off Dawson Road,
Benin City, Edo State.

DEDICATION

This Book is Specially Dedicated to GOD ALMIGHTY, for providing me with a Stronger Wings to Fly. He is indeed, ***"The Wind Beneath My Wings".***

FORWARD

It is with deep sense of appreciation and immense joy that I write the forward of this book which I know will be of great benefit to Lawyers, Judges, Law Lecturers, Law students, Magistrates and others who have interest in Probate matters.

The author, V. O. Ekomwerenren has used her experience as a Lawyer and a staff of the Probate Registry of the High Court of Justice, Edo State for over Ten years, together with her experience in the Litigation Department of the High Court to put this book together. It is a book that combines theory with practice as it relates to Probate and Administration of Estate in Nigeria.

The twenty-five chapter book covers the field and any Lawyer, Law Lecturer, Law Student or Judge who wants to find out or know more about Probate and Letters of Administration should have this book as it provides answers to some nagging questions on Probate related matters and Administration of Estate.

In an era where writing of Wills and depositing same at the Probate Registry is gaining so much relevance, coupled with the high rate of filing of cases in Court challenging Wills, this book will to a large extent be of much value to both Lawyers and Judges.

With the high rate of Judgments of Courts voiding the Will of the deceased Benin man as a result of the quarrel over who inherit the Igiogbe of a deceased Benin man, the question in the mind of most people is "should I write a Will"? Is there need for the writing of a Will when the Court can change the Will after the Testator's death?

From this book, it is discovered that the Wills Law Cap. 172 Vol. vi Laws of Defunct Bendel State of Nigeria 1976 as applicable in Edo State has not said a Benin man cannot write a Will but that the Will should be subject to the Customary Law relating thereto.

I have had the honour and privilege of reading through the manuscript of the book and I congratulate the author, a Legal Practitioner, a Judiciary staff and a mother for finding the time to write a very important book such as this.

I recommend the book to Legal Practitioners, Law Lecturers, Law Students and Judges as the book will be of immense benefit to them and their work.

Dr. James O. Otoghile
Deputy Chief Registrar (Litigation)
High Court of Justice,
Edo State.

PREFACE

The significance and imperativeness of the Probate Registry in our contemporary times cannot be over emphasized, having regards to the enormous responsibilities, function or roles played by the Probate Registry. The background to this book stems on the fact that there has now been more responsibilities on the Probate Registry of the Judiciary than it was some years back, and this calls for an in-depth understanding of the procedural methods and rules for granting Probate and Letters of Administration in respect of a deceased's estate. The Probate Registry of the High Court of Edo State was used as a case study in this book.

In line with the primary duty of a Court as guaranteed by the Constitution of the Federal Republic of Nigeria, 1999 (as amended)(1) and the High Court of Edo State (Civil Procedure) Rules,(2) the Court has the unfettered discretion to grant Probate and Letters of Administration, having regards to the rights of all persons interested in the estate, as well as the information made available before the Court.

By the operation of the above Laws, the Probate Registry (here in after referred to as "The Registry") of the High Court of Edo State is saddled with the responsibility of granting Probate and Letters of Administration in respect of a deceased's estate to interested persons. The Registry, usually under an Assistant Chief Registrar (ACR) or a Director, is directly answerable to the Probate Registrar (here in after referred to as "The Registrar"), who is the Chief Registrar of the Court.

The practice and procedure at the Registry of High Court of Edo State requires the following to be issued to the beneficiaries or members of the deceased family:

(1) Probate;
(2) Letters of Administration (Without Will);
(3) Letters of Administration (With Will Annexed);
(4) Resealing of Probate or Letters of Administration.

It is trite Law that on the death of a man, his wife, children or brothers have no legal right and cannot dispose of his property without Letters of Administration or Will duly admitted to Probate.(3) With regards to practice and procedure, relating to Probate and Administration, what then is Probate, Letters of Administration (Without Will), Letters of Administration (With Will Annexed), and Resealing of Probate or Letters of Administration.

Probate is the grant obtained by persons named in a testator's Will. Probate simply means the judicial procedure by which a testamentary document is established to be a valid Will; the proving of a Will to the satisfaction of the Court.(4) In the grant of Probate, the main concern of the Court is to grant Probate to the executors named in the Will to carry out the wishes of the testator.(5)

Letters of Administration (Without Will) are Letters granted to a person who has interest in the property or estate of a deceased person who died without making a Will and he is also referred to as Applicant. In the grant of Letters of Administration, the surviving spouse and children of the deceased take priority, having exclusive right to the estate of the deceased.

It is of importance to know that an Administrator derives his authority from the Letters of Administration. The authority an Administrator has is to manage the estate of the deceased's property on behalf of the beneficiaries.(6)

The grant obtained by persons interested in the testator's estate, other than the executors, is known as Letters of Administration (With Will Annexed). The Administration with the Will annexed, is a process of appointing Administrator in respect of a testator's estate, either because his Will does not name an executor or the named executor does not qualify.

Resealing simply means to reseal with the seal of a Court, the Probate or Letters of Administration earlier granted by a Court having jurisdiction in matters of Probate in a Commonwealth Country or by a High Court of another State.

For a better understanding, appreciation and ease of reference, it is imperative to know that a maker of a Will is called Testator (Male) /Testatrix (Female). The person named by a Testator to carry out his wishes, hold or distribute his property as directed in the Will is called Executor(7) (Male)/ Executrix (Female),while the person appointed by a Court to manage the assets and liabilities of an intestate is known as Administrator (Male)/ Administratrix (Female). In this book however, the terms "Testator", "Executor" and "Administrator" refer to both sexes.

There are two procedures for the grant of Probate of a Will. Probate may be granted either in common form or in solemn form.(8) Thus a grant can be taken out from the High Court in Solemn Form (that is, by way of litigation) or in Common Form (otherwise known as Common Form Business) through the Probate Registry of the High Court. Common Form Business, therefore, means the businesses of obtaining Probate and Administration where there is no contention as to the right thereto, including the passing of Probate and Administration through the Court in contentious cases where the contest has been terminated and all business of a non-contentious nature in matters of testacy and intestacy not being proceeding in any action and also the business of lodging caveats against the grants of Probate or Administration.[9]

Though the Registry of the High Court of Edo State is used as a case study in this book, however, non-contentious or common form probate business throughout Nigeria is substantially the same, hence, references are made to Probate Rules of High Court of Delta State (Civil Procedure) Rules, 2009 and High Court of Lagos State (Civil Procedure) Rules, 2012.[10] The framework of this book is divided into Twenty-Five chapters:

The first Chapter deals with the duties performed by the Registrar and the various sections within the Registry of the High Court of Edo State.

Chapter Two emphasizes how application for grant of Administration can be made and the mode of application.

The first set of Probate forms to be given to applicants to fill and return same are dealt with in Chapter Three.

Chapter Four is the importance of interview of applicants and the publication of application for grant.

Chapter Five talks about the Probate Estate, in other words, the type of the estate or property of the deceased the applicants seek to administer.

The second set of Probate forms given to applicants for grant of Administration is dealt with in Chapter Six.

The Estate Fee chargeable on the estate of a deceased and the Penal Sum attached thereto, is considered in Chapter Seven.

The types of Notices of Application for Grant under the Probate Rules and Persons to be served are discussed in Chapter Eight.

The procedural method of preparing Grant and the content of a Grant are spelt out in Chapter Nine.

How the personal representative of a deceased whose estate is less than ₦50,000 (Fifty Thousand Naira) or not more than, can gain access to such estate, is dealt with in Chapter Ten.

Financial Assistance made available to deceased's personal representative having challenges on how to raise the estate fee chargeable on the estate of the deceased, is discussed under Chapter Eleven.

Chapter Twelve talks about Wills' issues, among other things, Lodgment of Wills, Reading of Wills, Withdrawal and Revocation of deposited Wills, etc.

Chapter Thirteen deals with how Wills read are propounded or admitted to proof.

Some of the irregularities observed during the Examination of Wills before admitting them to proof and mode of clearing off such irregularities are discussed in Chapter Fourteen.

How Persons named in a Testator's Will can apply and prove the Will and also how to obtain grant in respect of a Codicil, is dealt with in Chapter Fifteen.

Instances where Administration With Will Annexed are made available to the personal representative of a deceased's estate are enumerated in Chapter Sixteen.

The various Grants classified as Limited also obtainable from the Court in truly Special Circumstances are discussed in Chapter Seventeen.

How Grants issued by Probate Registries outside a State in Nigeria or another State within Nigeria, in which a deceased person also left a part of his property is given Operational Force (Resealing), are discussed in Chapter Eighteen. Equally not left out in this Chapter is how to obtain documents to administer the assets of a deceased person which may be discovered after a Grant has previously been obtained.

Chapter Nineteen deals with the procedural method for Additional personal representatives and Joinder of an Administrator to existing Administrators.

The role and importance of Affidavits in Probate Matters is considered in Chapter Twenty.

How Searches in Probate Matters are conducted and how to obtain Certified True Copies of Probate Documents are dealt with in Chapter Twenty-One.

Chapter Twenty-Two and chapter Twenty-Three are devoted to the rules and procedure of opposing issue of a grant (that is, Notice of Prohibition, Caveat and Citation) to a particular applicant or to any body at all.

Chapter Twenty-Four deals with how the administration of the estate of a deceased person is said to be completed.

Chapter Twenty-Five, the last chapter talks about how to institute Probate Court Action.

V. O EKOMWERENREN
BENIN-CITY
2019

REFERENCES

(1) See sections 6 & 274 Constitution of the Federal Republic of Nigeria, 1999 (as amended).

(2) High Court of Edo State (Civil Procedure) Rules, 2018.

(3) See the case of Olora V. Adegbite (2013) 1 NWLR (pt. 1334) p.40.

(4) See the case of Nsefik V. Muna (2014) 2 NWLR (pt. 1490) p. 151.

(5) See the case of Motoh V, Motoh (2011) 16 NWLR (pt. 1274) p.474.

(6) See the case of ArijeV. Arije (2011) 13 NWLR (pt. 1264) p. 265.

(7) See the case of Mudashiru V. Abdullahi (2011) 7 NWLR (pt.1227) p.591.

(8) See the case of Nsefik V. Muna (2014), supra. For detailed Case Law Authorities on Administration of Estate, see Momodu, B., "Encyclopedia of Nigeria Case Law Principles and Authorities", Momodu B. Law Publishing, Benin-City, 2018, pgs. 11-17.

(9) See Mosanya, J. A., "Common Form Probate Business" Published by Mbeyi & Associates (Nig.) Ltd, Lagos, 2007, pgs. xiii-xiv.

(10) See Ors. 58 & 59 High Court of Edo State (Civil Procedure) Rules, 2018; Ors. 54 & 55 High Court of Delta State (Civil Procedure) Rules, 2009 and Ors. 57-60 High Court of Lagos State (Civil Procedure) Rules, 2012.

COMMENT

The Book titled PROBATE AND LETTERS OF ADMINISTRATION MADE EASY is an excellent Book with appropriate answers to many questions asked by the learned and the un-learned. It is a working handbook; quite educative, informative and instructive.

The author, a Lawyer went through the step by step process leading to the grant of Probate and Letters of Administration, from skills and experience she garnered while in the Probate Registry, hence her explanation and illustration is easy to grasp; she left no stone unturned.

I have the rare privilege of going through the manuscript of this Book. It touched every important area of Probate and Letters of Administration process. It is an asset for practicing Lawyers, Law Lecturers, Law Students, Judges and the Public in general.

I gladly recommend this Book for all.

Elder S. Odigie
Assistant Chief Registrar (Rtd)
(Former ACR In Charge Of Probate Registry)
High Court of Justice
Edo State
2019

APPRECIATION

I owe a huge debt of gratitude to Almighty God for making this Book a reality at last. As long as I live, I will continue to remember and pray for the soul of my Mother: Late Madam Alice Aghayere Obazuaye. Her being a "SPECIAL MOTHER" made a difference in my life.

Special Thanks to Elder Sunny Odigie, who was the Assistant Chief Registrar in Charge of Probate Registry during my service in the Registry. He planted in me the idea of this book, many years ago. It also gives me a great pleasure to thank Dr. James O. Otoghile for his support, contributions and for making out time to proofread the manuscript of this book along with Elder Sunny Odigie and Emwinghare Edokpaigbe, Esq. My thanks also go to Jatto Oyekpen, who gave this Book its Title.

Grateful thanks are due to O. A. Omonuwa, SAN, Professor Daniel Okunbor, Eghosa Chinyere Okunbor, Patrick O. Ebhodaghe, Hart Onoko, Lilian Onoko, Josiah Odiale, Amaka Odiale, Emmanuel E. Ativie, Esq., Emwinghare Edokpaigbe, Esq., I.D. Iredia-Osifo, Esq., for their suggestions and encouragement. I remain grateful to Modupe Irorere and Anthony Uwota in typing the manuscript. I accept responsibility for any error in the book.

Finally, I thank my husband, Ikponmwosa Ekomwerenren, Esq., my lovely children Osasenaga, Iwinosa and my ever caring brothers, Dr. Alex Nosa Obasuyi, Dr. Henry Omobude-Igiebor and Frank Obayagbona, for their encouragement, understanding and support.

V. O. EKOMWERENREN
2019

ABBREVIATIONS

All NLR	All Nigeria Law Report
AEL (Bendel)	Administration of Estate Law, Cap.2 Vol. 1, Laws of Defunct Bendel State of Nigeria 1976 as Applicable in Edo State
(DELTA) 2009	High Court of Delta State (Civil Procedure) Rules, 2009
EDO HCLR	Edo High Court Law Report
(EDO) 2018	High Court of Edo State (Civil Procedure) Rules, 2018
(LAGOS) 2012	High Court of Lagos State (Civil Procedure) Rules, 2012
MRSCJ	Monthly Report of Supreme Court Judgment
NSCQR	Nigerian Supreme Court Quarterly Report
NWLR	Nigerian weekly Law Report
Or	Order
R	Rule
WRN	Western Report of Nigeria

CASES CITED

TABLE OF CONTENTS

Chapter Seventeen:

Chapter Eighteen:

CHAPTER ONE

THE DUTIES PERFORMED BY THE REGISTRAR AND THE VARIOUS SECTIONS WITHIN THE REGISTRY.

The Probate Registry of the High Court of Edo State has the entire State as its jurisdiction of operation and is headed by the Probate Registrar. The Registry is divided into the following sections namely:

i. First Set Of Forms Section
ii. Correspondence Section
iii. Litigation Section
iv. Account Section
v. Typing Pool Section
vi. Archive Section

THE PROBATE REGISTRAR

The Registrar being the administrative head in charge of the Registry, it is his duty to receive applications for grant of Probate or Letters of Administration in respect of a deceased's estate and all applications on other matters connected therewith.(1)

Upon receiving such applications for grant, the Registrar will not allow any grant to be issued until all inquiries which he may deem fit to make have been answered to his satisfaction.(2)

It is the duty of the Registrar to require proof of the identity of the deceased or of the applicant for the grant of Probate or Letters of Administration beyond that which is in the application or probate forms filled and filed.(3)

He must not issue grant within twenty-one (21) days of the publication of application for grant of Letters of Administration. Also, he must not issue grant of Probate or Letters of

Administration with Will annexed within seven (7) days and grant of Letters of Administration without Will within fourteen (14) days of the death of the deceased.[4] He must ensure that the person to whom Letters of Administration is granted give a bond with responsible Sureties,[5] he must avoid error and fraud in granting Probate or Letters of Administration.[6]

The Registrar is the custodian of all Wills and he sign on behalf of the Court, all Probate or Letters of Administration [7]. He receive and process application for the Resealing of Probate or Letters of Administration granted either by a Court having jurisdiction in matters of Probate in a Commonwealth Country or by a High Court of another State[8].

It is the duty of the Registrar to ascertain the value of property to be covered by the grant sought.[9]

FIRST SET OF FORMS SECTION

This is the section where you obtain and submit application for grant of Letters of Administration, especially without Will. It is the duty of the officer in charge of this section to issue the first set of Probate forms once such application is approved by the Registrar and if there is no previous application pending in respect of the deceased's estate. The first set of forms comprises of:

i. Application for Probate or Letters of Administration
ii. Inventory
iii. Declaration as to Next-of-Kin
iv. Bank Certificate

These forms are usually issued to applicant by a forwarding letter.

CORRESPONDENCE SECTION

The officers in this section are in charge of treating all letters relating to correspondence duties, that is, outward and inward mails. In other words, they receive letters and applications on behalf of the Registrar. This include application for reading of Wills, Certified True Copy, Searches and confirmation of grant of Letters of Administration (with or without Will annexed). They also dispatch Second Set of Probate forms, letters to Pension Boards, Pension Managers, Ministry of Lands etc.

LITIGATION SECTION

The officers in this section are in charge of Court Representation and related matters involving the Registrar. They issue forms for grant of Probate, prepare the second set of probate forms, administer Oaths, supervise the compilation of legal notice, draft letters, cross-check draft or typed documents. They also conduct interview for applicants and ensure proper completion of the second set of forms before payment of estate fees by applicants.

ACCOUNT SECTION

The officers in this section are called Probate Cashiers. They collect all revenue and payment made in the Registry and promptly issue receipts under the appropriate head or sub-head for such. They ensure proper endorsement of all money in the relevant forms or documents. Payment of all revenue collected is made into designated bank accounts. The Cashier renders monthly returns of all payments and deposits to the Registrar or any other appropriate officer.

TYPING POOL SECTION

This is where all official letters and documents relating to Probate Matters are typed. It is the duty of officers in this section to ensure that all official letters and documents are correctly typed with minimum delay.

ARCHIVE SECTION

This is where all files relating to Probate Matters are properly arranged and kept, both pending and concluded matters. It is the duty of the officers in this section to monitor the movement of all files and to be able to trace their where about at any given time.

REFERENCES

(1) Or.58 R.1(1) & Or.59R.6(1) (Edo) 2018; Or.54 R.1(1) & Or.55 R.6(1) (Delta) 2009; Or.57 R.1(1) (Lagos) 2012 and Section 20 AEL (Bendel) 1976.

(2) Or.58 R.12(1) & Or.59 R.9(1) & R.(24) (Edo) 2018; Or.54 R.12(1) & Or.55 R.9(1) & R.24 (Delta) 2009 and Or.59 R.6 (Lagos) 2012, supra.

(3) Or.58 R.9 & Or.59 R.9(2) (Edo) 2018; Or.54 R.9 & Or.55 R.9(2) (Delta) 2009 and Or.57 R.5(2) & R.8 (Lagos) 2012, supra.

(4) Or.58 R.1(3) & Or.59 R.9(3) (Edo) 2018; Or.54 R.1(3) & Or.55 R. 9(3) (Delta) and Or.57 R.1(2). NOTE: Under the Lagos Rules, no grant of administration with the Will annexed shall issue within fourteen (14) days of the death of the deceased and no grant of administration without the Will annexed shall issue within twenty-one (21) days of such death.

(5) Or.58 R.30(1) (Edo) 2018; Or.54 R.30(1) (Delta) 2009 and Or.59 R.3(1) (Lagos) 2012, supra.

(6) Or.58 R.12(2) & Or.59 R.24 (Edo) 2018; Or.54 R.12(2) & Or.55 R.24 (Delta) 2009 and Or.59 R.6 (Lagos) 2012, supra.

(7) Or.58 R.44 (Edo) 2018; Or.54 R.44 (Delta) 2009 and Or.59 R.19 (Lagos) 2012, supra.

(8) Or.59 R.55 (Edo) 2018; Or.55 R.55 (Delta) 2009 and Or.58 R.26 (Lagos) 2012, supra.

(9) Or.58 R.29(2) (Edo) 2018; Or.54 R.29(2) (Delta) 2009 and Or.59 R.1 (Lagos) 2012, supra.

CHAPTER TWO

APPLICATION FOR GRANT OF ADMINISTRATION: HOW TO APPLY AND MODE OF APPLICATION

Administration in relation to any estate can be defined as the management and settlement of the estate of an intestate deceased or a testator who has no Executor, by person legally appointed and supervised by the Court.[(1)]

Administration of an estate involves realizing the movable assets of a deceased person and paying out of them any debts or other claims against the estate. It also involves the division and distribution of what remains. [(2)]

There are various kinds of Administration in respect of a deceased's estate; however, the most commonly granted Administration in the Registry comprises:

i. Letters of Administration (without Will).
ii. Letters of Administration (with Will Annexed).

LETTERS OF ADMINISTRATION (WITHOUT WILL)

Letters of Administration (without Will) is granted in respect of the estate of a deceased who died intestate. A person is said to have died intestate if he lives no valid Will at death. In granting of Letters of Administration the surviving spouse and the children of the deceased take priority having exclusive right to the estate of the deceased. A person who intends to administer the estate of the deceased is referred to as applicant.

Thus, the formal document issued by a Court to appoint the Administrator in such estate is called Letters of Administration or Administration Letters. A person appointed by the Court to manage the assets and liabilities of an intestate is known as Administrator.

LETTERS OF ADMINISTRATION (WITH WILL ANNEXED)

Letters of Administration (with Will annexed) is granted in respect of estate of a Testator, either because the Will does not name an Executor or where all the Executors named in the Will predeceased the Testator or the named Executor does not qualify. This type of grant is made to persons beneficially interested in the Testator's estate.

A Testator is a person who has made a Will and a person named by a Testator to carry out the provisions in the Testator's Will is known as Executor, while a person who receives a gift from a deceased estate is called a Beneficiary.

HOW TO APPLY FOR GRANT

The High Court of Edo State (Civil Procedure) Rules, 2018 provides thus:

> *"subject to the provision of rules 39 and 40, when any person subject to the jurisdiction of the Court dies, all petitions for the granting of any letters of administration of the estate of the deceased person with or without Will attached, and all application on other matters connected therewith, shall be made to the Probate Registrar of the Court of Benin City."*[(3)]

Therefore anyone who wishes to obtain grant of Letters of Administration must apply to the Registrar. The applicant must bring a formal application to the Registry. The application must contain the full names of the deceased, the place and date of death, a photocopy of the medical certificate of death or a certificate of proof of death is also attached. All necessary inquires will be made and answered satisfactorily to know whether the applicant is entitled to be granted Letters of Administration or not.

MODE OF APPLICATION

Application for grant of administration can be made through legal representation or personal representation.

LEGAL REPRESENTATION

A Legal Practitioner can apply for Probate forms on behalf of a client. Such client must be over eighteen (18) years of age.

Thus:

"(1) A person applying for a grant through a legal practitioner, may apply otherwise than by post at the Probate Registry.

(2) Every legal practitioner through whom an application for a grant is made, shall give the address of his place of business within jurisdiction".[(4)]

PERSONAL REPRESENTATION

A Personal Applicant may apply for a grant without employing a legal practitioner.[(5)] Therefore, a widow, widower, son, daughter, brother, sister, cousin, nephew, niece, father, mother, uncle, aunt, grand-child, grand-parents, executor etc can personally apply for Probate forms in order to administer the estate of their deceased loved ones. Such Applicant must be over eighteen (18) years of age and Probate forms can only be issue to the person that signed the application form or application letter.

It is the duty of a Personal Applicant to produce death certificate of the deceased or such other evidence of the death as the Registrar may approve and also supply all information necessary for the filling of forms.[6]

However, no personal application can be proceeded with if an application has already been made by a Legal Practitioner on behalf of the Applicant and has not been withdrawn. And also if it becomes necessary to bring the matter before the Court on Motion or by Action.[7]

PERSONS ENTITLED TO BE GRANTED LETTERS OF ADMINISTRATION

Persons entitled to be granted Letters of Administration are as follows:

1. Husband or wife of the deceased;
2. Children of the deceased or the surviving issues of the children or child who died in the lifetime of the deceased;
3. Father or mother of the deceased;
4. Brothers or sisters of the deceased of whole blood and the children of such brothers or sisters who died in the lifetime of the deceased;
5. Brothers or sisters of half-blood of the deceased or the children of any such brother or sister who died in the lifetime of the deceased;
6. Grandfather or grandmother of the deceased;
7. Uncles or aunts of whole blood or their children;
8. Creditors of the deceased;
9. Administrator general (where all the preceding) fail.

REFERENCES

1. Garner, B.A., "Black's Law Dictionary" U.S.A, Thomson Reuters West Publishing Co. Ltd Ninth Edition, 2009, pg.49.
2. Ibid.
3. Or.58 R.1(1) & Or.59 R.6(1) (Edo) 2018; Or.54 R.1(1) & Or.55 R.6(1) (Delta) 2009; Or.57 R.1(1) (Lagos) 2012, and section 20 AEL (Bendel) 1976, supra.
4. Or.59 R.7 (Edo) 2018; Or.55 R.7 (Delta) 2009 and Or.57 R.4 (Lagos) 2012, Supra.
5. Or.59 R.8(1)(2) (Edo) 2018; Or.55 R8.(1)(2) (Delta) 2009 and Or.57 R.3(1)(2) (Lagos) 2012, supra.
6. Or.59 R.8(5)(6) ibid; Or.55 R.8(5)(6) ibid and Or.57 R. 3(5)(6) ibid.
7. Or.59 R.8(3) ibid; Or.55 R.8(3) ibid and Or.57 R.3(3) ibid.

CHAPTER THREE

PROBATE FIRST SET OF FORMS

The First sets of Probate forms issued to an applicant who apply for grant of Letters of Administration include the following:

i. Application for Probate or Letters of Administration
ii. Inventory
iii. Declaration as to Next-of-Kin
iv. Bank Certificate

These forms are issued to an applicant by a forwarding letter which contains all necessary information as regard filing fees, publication fees and required documents to be attached to completed form.(1) It is important to know that two passport photograph of each of the applicants are also attached to completed forms.

APPLICATION FOR PROBATE OR LETTERS OF ADMINISTRATION

This form contains the following:

i. The full names of the deceased;
ii. The village and Local Government Area where the deceased hailed from;
iii. The State of Origin (other than Edo State);
iv. The place and date of death;
v. The full names and addresses of the applicants;
vi. The relationship between the deceased and the applicants;
vii. The estimated value of the real and personal property in respect of which a grant of administration is sought.

It is pertinent to note that the date of filing this form is usually the said date on the Grant which the applicants are deemed to have applied for Letters of Administration.[2]

INVENTORY

This is a declaration form for personal and real property of the deceased within the possession or knowledge of the applicants.[3]

It also contain the full names of the deceased, village, Local Government Area, State of Origin and the deceased fixed place of abode within the jurisdiction of the Court.

Where real properties are declared, the location of the properties must be within the jurisdiction of the Court.

DECLARATION AS TO NEXT-OF-KIN

This form contains the names of the deceased, his immediate and extended family.[4] The deceased's immediate and extended family information required on this form are:

i. The names and address of the spouse;
ii. The type of marriage and the date the marriage was contracted;
iii. Names of children and their mothers;
iv. Ages of the children;
v. Names and address of the parents;
vi. Names and addresses of brothers and sisters;
vii. Name and address of person whom minor children live with.

BANK CERTIFICATE

This form is to inform the deceased's bank that the applicant whose name appeared on the bank certificate has the authority to enquire on behalf of the Registrar any sum outstanding to the credit or debit of the deceased.[(5)]

The form must be endorsed by a Bank.[(6)] However, there are cases where the deceased's statement of account can suffice. It contains the deceased's file number, issuing date, full names of the deceased and the applicant. It must be signed and stamped by a designated officer of the Registry before taken to deceased's bank.

The above mentioned forms are expected to be filled and returned.

REFERENCES

(1) See Appendix 26 for specimen of Letter forwarding first set of Probate forms.

(2) See Appendix 15 for specimen of Application for Probate or Letters of Administration Form.

(3) See Appendix 23 for specimen of Inventory form.

(4) See Appendix 22 for specimen of Declaration as to Next-of-Kin form.

(5) See Appendix 17 for specimen of Bank Certificate form.

(6) NOTE: Where a deceased person has no Bank Account, a sworn Affidavit to that effect can suffice.

CHAPTER FOUR

INTERVIEW OF APPLICANTS AND PUBLICATION OF APPLICATION FOR GRANT

INTERVIEW OF APPLICANTS

After the completion of the First set of Probate forms, applicants for grant of Administration are made to appear before an authorized officer of the Registry for an interview.

It is the duty of the interviewing officer to ensure that the forms are properly filled and discrepancy in the deceased's names, place of death or date of death, if any, are resolved. Also ensure that the applicants before him are those whose passport photographs are affixed. This interview is in line with Probate Rules.

Thus:

> *"The Court shall require evidence, in addition to that offered by the applicant, where additional evidence in that behalf seems to the Court necessary or desirable, in regard to the identity of the deceased or of the applicant or in regard to the relationship of the applicant to the deceased, or in regard to any persons in existence with a right equal or prior to that of the applicant to the grant of probate or administration sought by the applicant, or in regard to any other matter which may be considered by the Court relevant to the question whether the applicant is the proper person to whom the grant should be made:*
>
> *Provided that the Court may refuse the grant unless the applicant produces the required evidence on those points or any of them as required by the Court".*[(1)]

The purpose of interview is to enable the Registrar determine whether the applicants are the proper persons to whom the grant should be made. In other words, to investigate by evidence the identity of the deceased, that of the applicants and the relationship of the applicant to the deceased or in regard to the existence with a right equal or prior to that of the applicants to the grant sought. Also to prevent to a large extent error and fraud in the process of granting Administration.(2)

Once the interviewing officer is satisfied with the answers or evidence provided by the applicants to all inquiries and the discrepancy, if any, resolved, applicants are then allowed to pay filing and publications fees. Thereafter, the administration of oath on the relevant forms by applicants and the interviewing officer, acting as the Commissioner for Oaths.

PUBLICATION OF APPLICATION FOR GRANT

Publication of Application for grant is also termed "Legal Notice". It is a printed announcement that is intended to reach particular persons or the public.

In Probate matters, publication of application means the process of making known to the public the application for grant of Letters of Administration in respect of a named deceased's estate. The purpose of publication of application is to alert the general public and especially the people in the community or the place of abode where the deceased lived and died within the jurisdiction of the Court, who may be interested in the deceased's estate that some persons have applied for a grant of Letters of Administration. It also help to check-mate and reduce possible deception on the part of applicants.

Thus:

> *"The Court shall, however, afford as great a facility for the obtaining of letters of administration as is consistent with due regard to the prevention of error and fraud."(3)*

Thus, when completed First set of Probate forms have been checked and are in order, applicants for grant of Administration having been interviewed, filing and publication fees paid, signature of applicants obtained and the administration of Oath by the interviewing officer, the application will then be published in a newspaper. The Nigerian Observer Newspaper is the official newspaper for publication of application and the notice is usually for twenty-one (21) days. Immediately after publication, file is opened for the deceased's estate matter.

TYPES OF PUBLICATION

There are two types of publication available in the Registry, namely:

i. Multiple publication
ii. Single publication.

MULTIPLE PUBLICATION

This is the advertisement of a compilation of various applications for grant of Letters of Administration received by the Registrar within a short period of time.

This type of publication is usually done once or twice monthly depending on the turnout of applications in a particular month. The publication fee is relatively cheaper than the single publication.

SINGLE PUBLICATION

This is the advertisement of a single application for grant of Letters of Administration. In this type of publication, the applicants must be willing to pay for one quarter page advert of the newspaper. The advantage of this publication is that the advertisement is done the next day or immediately after the payment of publication fee, unlike the multiple publication where the application stay for days or weeks before publication.

It is of importance to know that the amount collected for Publication of Application for Grant is made in cash.

REFERENCES

(1) Or.58 R.9 (Edo) 2018; Or.54 R.9 (Delta) 2009 and Or.57 R.8 (Lagos) 2012, supra.

(2) Or.59 R.24 & Or.58 R.12 (Edo) 2018; Or.55 R.24 & Or. 54 R.12 (Delta) 2009 and Or.57 R.5 (Lagos) 2012, supra.

(3) Or.58 R.12(2) (Edo) 2018; Or.54 R.12(2) (Delta) 2009 and Or.59 R.6 (Lagos) 2012, supra.

CHAPTER FIVE

PROBATE ESTATE

A deceased's property subject to administration by a personal representative is known as Probate Estate or Probate Property [1]. Estate means the property that one leaves after death; the collective assets and liabilities of a dead person.[2]Estate can also be defined as the amount, degree, nature and quality of a person's interest in land or other property. Property is the right to possess, use and enjoy a determinate thing (either a tract of land or a chattel); right of ownership.[3]

In other words, all the money and property that a deceased owned, such as vacant land, buildings, chattels, shares and debts due to him are his estate. Therefore Probate Estate comprises property owned by the deceased at the time of death and property acquired by the deceased estate at or after the time of death.

Thus, after the publication of application for grant of Letters of Administration, the declarations on the inventory form filed, as to the estate of the deceased the applicants intend to administer determine the next line of action to be taken.

TYPES OF PROBATE ESTATE

The total of the personal and real property of the deceased is referred to as the Estate of the Deceased. Thus in this book and for ease of reference, declarations on inventory form which make up the estate of the deceased are divided into two (2) groups, that is:

(a) Personal Estate/Personal Property

(b) Real Estate/Real Property

PERSONAL ESTATE/PERSONAL PROPERTY

Personal Property is any movable or intangible thing that is subject to ownership and not classified as real property [4]. The personal estates of a deceased include:

i. Money in bank;[5]
ii. Money found at home;
iii. Stock in trade; [6]
iv. Chattels [7]
v. Death benefits or Debts due to the deceased [8]

REAL ESTATE /REAL PROPERTY

A deceased's real estate include:

i. Empty plot
ii. Houses[9]
iii. Uncompleted building
iv. Farm land and connected buildings used for agricultural purposes.

AFTERMATH OF PUBLICATION

If after publication of application and there is no caveat or notice to prohibit grant and if any, but was resolved and cleared off or lifted, the following are likely to be done:

(i) Where the applicants intend to administer money in deceased's bank accounts only or fund with Pension Managers only or shares owned by the deceased in various companies only or both money in bank, shares and fund with pension managers; provided the most recent shares certificates, dividend slips or central security clearing system (CSCS) account print out and the retirement savings statement of account are filed along with the First sets of Probate forms or made available to the Registrar before or immediately after the publication of application, then the second set of probate forms will be issue to applicants.

(ii) Where the applicants intend to administer Death Benefit or debts due to the deceased, that is:

(a) Where the deceased died in service either at the Federal, State or Local Government level;
(b) Where the deceased was retired but yet to be paid his pension and gratuity;
(c) Where the deceased had started receiving pension and gratuity after retirement, but was owned some arrears;
(d) Where the deceased had savings with Pension Manager and the most recent Retirement Savings Statement of account was not filed along with the First set of Probate forms or made available before or immediately after publication of application;

Then a letter calling for the figures or amount representing the deceased's entitlements, written and signed by an authorized officer on behalf of the Registrar is issued to the applicants for onward delivery or send by post to the particular Pension Board or Pension Manager in charge of the deceased's entitlement. If the deceased died in service, a copy of the said letter will be forwarded to the deceased's last place of work.

(iii) Where real properties are declared, their location must be within the jurisdiction of the Court.(10) And a letter is addressed to the Permanent Secretary,

Ministry of Lands, requesting for assessment and valuation report on the deceased's real properties listed in the said letter.

It is possible for applicants to administer or declare on the inventory form filed both personal and real estate at the same time.

IMPORTANCE OF REPLY TO LETTERS CALLING FOR FIGURES AND VALUATION REPORT ON REAL PROPERTIES

It is the duty of the Registrar to ascertain the value of the property to be covered by the Letters of Administration.(11) Therefore, reply to letters calling for figures, valuation report on real properties, knowing the value of deceased's shares in the various companies, money in banks, etc, enable the Registrar to ascertain the value of property to be covered by the grant sought. In some cases involving savings with Pension Managers, the production of the retirement savings statement of account in lieu of reply to the letter calling for figures can suffice.

Once the Registrar can ascertain the gross value of the estate of the deceased, only then will the Second Set of Probate forms be prepared and issued to Applicants.

REFERENCES

(1) Garner, B. A., "Black's Law Dictionary", supra pg. 1322.
(2) See the case of Carew V. Oguntokun (2011) 5 NWLR (pt.1220) p. 376.
(3) Garner, B. A., "Black's Law Dictionary", supra pgs. 626 and 1335, respectively.
(4) Ibid, pg.1337.
(5) That is, Money in Saving Account, Current Account and Fixed Deposit, etc
(6) For example, Shares, Bond etc.
(7) This include Car, Ship, Boat, Jewelry, etc.
(8) That is, Pension, Gratuity, Arrears of Pension and Gratuity, Fund with Pension Managers or Insurance Companies, etc.
(9) For example, Bungalow, Storey Building, Duplex, Sky Scrapper, etc.
(10) See Appendix 29 for a specimen of letter calling for figures.
(11) Within Edo State.
(12) Or.58 R.29(2) (Edo) 2018; Or.54 R.29(2) (Delta) 2009 and Or.59 R.1 (Lagos) 2012, supra.

CHAPTER SIX

SECOND SET OF PROBATE FORMS

In grant of Letters of Administration, upon the expiration of the Legal Notice, provided no caveat or notice to prohibit grant filed, and if any, was resolved and cleared off or lifted and the Registrar has ascertain the gross value of the deceased estate to be covered by the grant sought,[(1)] the Second set of Probate forms are prepared with a copy of the Legal Notice attached and is issued by a forwarding letter to applicants, with a request to proceed to the Magistrate's Court, along with their Sureties. [(2)]If applicable, Notice of Application to persons in existence with a right equal or prior to that of the applicants to the grant sought, is issued as well.[(3)]

The second set of forms consist of the following:

i. Oath for Administration;
ii. Administration Bond;
iii. Justification of Sureties;
iv. Suretyship form.

The forwarding letter for issuing the above forms is addressed to the Chief Magistrate in the area where the applicants live within the jurisdiction of the Court and is signed by a senior officer of the Registry. The content of the letter include information regarding the penal sum, estate fee, filing fees for each of the form as well as the amount payable for oath at the Magistrate's Court.[(4)]

EXECUTION OF SECOND SET OF PROBATE FORMS

At the Magistrate's Court, the forms are filled by an authorized officer. The Sureties are presented before the Chief Magistrate, who examines their means and approves the suitability of the Sureties for such exercise. Once the Sureties are approved,[(5)] payment for oath and signing of the various forms are done.

The Oath for Administration form is to be signed by the applicants only.[(6)] Whereas, the Administration Bond form is signed by all the applicants and the two Sureties.[(7)] While the Justification of Sureties and Suretyship forms are signed by the two sureties only.[(8)]

The completed and signed forms are thereafter return to the Registry for filing along with the reply to Notice of Application, if any and a bank draft in favour of the Registrar, with the amount chargeable as the estate fee.[(9)] Before the payment of estate fee, the forms are checked by an officer of the Registry to ensure proper completion and signing of the forms. If they are in order, the documents are arranged in the deceased's file and payment is made. After payment, the Suretyship forms are endorsed by the Registrar as final approval of the Sureties.

By virtue of Paragraph 21 of the Second Schedule of the High Court of Justice Edo State (Civil Procedure) Rules, 2018, the 10% (ten percent) Probate Fee in respect of Pensioners Entitlement is to be deducted at the point of payment.

In other words, Pensioners Entitlements could be processed by their Next-of-Kin but the 10% (Ten percent) Probate Fee would be deducted at the point of payment and remitted to the Registry by the relevant Organ of Government.[(10)]

REFERENCES

(1) "Gross Value" in relation to any estate, means the value of the estate without deduction for debts, encumbrances, funeral expenses or estate duty- see Or.59 R.80(2) (Edo) 2018; Or.55 R.80(2) Delta 2009 and Or.60 R.23(2) (Lagos) 2012, supra.

(2) Two Sureties are usually required so as to limit the liability of the Sureties- see Or.58 R.30(4) (Edo) 2018, supra.

(3) Not in all cases is Notice of Application for grant to persons entitled to grant, other than the applicants to the grant sought, is issued.

(4) See Appendix 27 for specimen of Letter forwarding the second set of Probate forms.

(5) The final approval of Sureties is done by the Registrar- see Or.58 R.30(1) (Edo) 2018; Or.54 R.30(1) (Delta) 2009 and Or.59 R.3(1) (Lagos) 2012, supra.

(6) See Appendice 40 & 41 for specimen of Oath For Administration form.

(7) See Appendix 1 for specimen of Administration Bond form.

(8) See Appendice24& 16 for specimen of Justification of Sureties and Application for Suretyship forms.

(9) For estate fee above 5,000 (Five Thousand Naira).

(10) See Executive Order No. 1 dated 1st day of August, 2018, issued by the Executive Governor of Edo State, His Excellency, Godwin Nogheghase Obaseki. See also, Administration of Estate Fee (Deduction At Source) Practice Direction dated 21st day of September, 2018, issued by Honourable Justice Esohe Frances Ikponmwen, FCJEI, Chief Judge of Edo State.

CHAPTER SEVEN

ESTATE FEE AND PENAL SUM

ESTATE FEE (ESTATE DUTY)

Estate fee (Estate Duty) is a tax imposed on the principal value of all property that passed on death.[1] In other words, Estate fee is the amount chargeable by law, on the estate of a deceased sought to be administered by persons interested. It is the duty of the Registrar to ascertain the value of the property to be covered by the Administration. Also, it is the duty of every applicant for a grant of Probate or Letters of Administration to file a true declaration of all the personal property of the deceased and the value thereof[2].

Thus, enquiry through bank certificate of any amount outstanding to the credit or debit of the deceased, requesting for shares certificate, dividend slips, central security clearing system account (CSCS) printout, letter calling for figures and valuation report on real properties, are done to enable the Registrar know the gross value of the estate of the deceased. Once the gross value is known, assessment of estate fee becomes fixable and easy.

The estate fee comprises 10% (ten per cent) of the value of the taxable estate of the deceased, which exceeds ₦50,000.00 (Fifty Thousand Naira).[3] It is important to note that where any property is declared to be owned partly by the deceased and another or other persons, the Deed of Partition or Deed of Conveyance or Certificate of Title by which the property was conveyed into the joint names must be produced to the Registrar. If the property is held as tenants-in-common, the share belonging to the deceased will form part of his estate, devolve under his Will or intestacy and will be accordingly assessed. In other words estate fee will only be charged on the deceased's severable share of the property.[4]

Payment of estate fee above N5,000.00 (Five Thousand Naira) is made in Bank Draft in the name of the Probate Registrar, High Court of Edo State. The Bank Draft is then presented to the Probate Cashier, who in turn issues receipt to the payer.

PENAL SUM

The Applicants for grant of Letters of Administration are made to give a bond in favour of the Registrar with two Sureties.[5]

Therefore:

> *"The person to whom administration is granted shall give a bond, with two or more responsible sureties, to the Probate Registrar of the Court, conditioned for duly collecting, getting in and administering the personal property of the deceased, such sureties to be to the satisfaction of the Probate Registrar."*[6]

The amount on such Bond is known as the Penal Sum. Thus a Surety undertakes that if the condition of the Bond is broken, the Surety will be liable in a penal sum, which usually, is twice the gross value of the estate of the deceased declared on the inventory form filed.

Thus:

> *"The bond shall be in a penalty of double the amount under which the personal estate of the deceased is sworn, unless the Court, in any case, thinks it expedient to reduce the amount."*[7]

The gross value in relation to any estate means the value of the estate without deduction for debts, encumbrances, funeral expenses or estate duty.(8) For instance, if the gross value of the estate of a deceased declared on the inventory form is N500,000.00 (Five Hundred Thousand Naira), the penal sum will be N1,000,000.00 (One Million Naira). Thus, both Sureties will be made to enter into a Bond of ₦1,000,000,00 (One Million Naira).

ASSIGNMENT OF BOND

The Registrar has power to enforce any Administration Bond or assign it to some other person.(9)

Where it appears to the satisfaction of the Registrar that the condition of an Administration Bond has been broken, he may assign such bond to some other person, who is entitle to sue in his own name to recover as trustee for all persons interested in the deceased's estate, the full amount recoverable in respect of the breach of the condition.

Thus:

> *"The Probate Registrar may on being satisfied that the condition of the bond has been broken, assign the same to some person, and that person may there upon sue on the bond in his own name as if it had been originally given to him instead of the Probate Registrar and may recover thereon as trustee for persons interested the full amount recoverable in respect of any breach of the bond."*(10)

REFERENCES

(1) Garner, B. A., "Black's Law Dictionary", supra pg. 581
(2) Or.58 R.11 & Or.59 R.23 (Edo) 2018; Or.54 R.11 & Or.55 R.23 (Delta) 2009 and Or.59 R.2 (Lagos) 2012, supra.
(3) See Paragraph 21 of the Second Schedule High Court of Edo State (Civil Procedure) Rules, 2018.
(4) Mosanya, J. A., "Common Form Probate Business", supra pgs. 243 & 244. NOTE: Tenancy in common simply implies a separate individual ownership of an undivided share by each of the tenants.
(5) A Bond is a written agreement or promise that is against the Law to break.
(6) Or.58 R.30 (1) (Edo) 2018; Or.54 R. 30(1) (Delta) 2009; Or.59 R.3 (1) (Lag0s) 2012 and section 31(1) AEL (Bendel) 1976, supra.
(7) Or.58 R.30(3) ibid; Or.54 R.30(3) ibid and Or.59 R.3(3)ibid.
(8) Or.59 R.80 (2) (Edo) 2018; Or.55 R.80 (2) (Delta) 2009 and Or.60 R.23 (2) (Lagos) 2012, supra.
(9) Section 31(2) AEL (Bendel) 1976.
(10) Or.58 R.31 (Edo) 2018; Or.54 R.31 (Delta) 2009; Or.59 R.5 (Lagos) 2012 and section 31 AEL (Bendel) 1976, supra.

CHAPTER EIGHT

NOTICE OF APPLICATION

The Registrar may refuse a grant of Letters of Administration until all persons interested in the estate of the deceased are given due notice.[1] A person having a property right[2] in or claim against a thing such as a trust or deceased's estate is deemed to be interested person in the administration of such trust or estate[3].

Thus:

> *"Where it appears to the Court that some person or persons other than the applicant may have at least an equal right with the applicant to the grant sought, the Court may refuse the grant until due notice of the application has been given to such other person or persons and an opportunity given for such person or persons to be heard in regard to the application:*
>
> > *Provided that the Court may in its discretion refuse the grant unless and until all persons entitled to the grant in priority to the applicant, shall have expressly renounced their prior right."*[4]

By the provision of the above Rule, Notice of Application to persons entitled to grant of Letters of Administration are of two categories:

i. Notice to person or persons having an "EQUAL RIGHT" with the applicants to the grant sought
ii. Notice to person or persons having a "PRIOR RIGHT" over the applicants to the grant sought.

PREPARATION OF NOTICE OF APPLICATION AND MODE OF SERVICE

The information filed on the Declaration as to Next-Of-Kin form is of vital importance in determining whether both or either of the Notice of Application will be served.

The Notice of application to person having an equal right or a prior right is typed, signed by an officer of the Registry, addressed and served on the person entitled to grant.[(5)]It is issued to applicants to the grant sought for onward delivery to the person served.[(6)]

It is important to note that Notice of Application can only be served on persons above eighteen (18) years of age and there are cases where both notices are served in respect of the estate of a deceased.

CONTENT OF NOTICE OF APPLICATION

A Notice of Application to be served on persons entitled to grant other than the applicants to the grant sought must contain the following:

i. The deceased's file number
ii. The name of the deceased
iii. The names of the applicants to the grant sought
iv. The relationship between the deceased and the applicants
v. The date the notice was signed.
vi. The names of the persons to be served.
vii. Signature of an authorized officer[(7)].

In Notice of Application to person having equal right with the applicants, the person served is informed that the applicants whose names appeared on the notice have applied for grant of

Letters of Administration in respect of the estate of the deceased and should let the Registrar know within fourteen (14) days of service whether or not the person served has any objection to the grant sought being made to the said applicants[8].

Whereas in Notice of Application to person having a prior right over the applicants, the person served is informed of his right which takes precedence over the applicants' right to the grant sought and should let the Registrar know within fourteen (14) days of service whether or not he intend to exercise such right [9].

CATEGORIES OF NOTICE OF APPLICATION

NOTICE OF APPLICATION TO PERSON HAVING EQUAL RIGHT WITH APPLICANTS

In relation to property right, a right is the interest, claim or ownership that one has in tangible or intangible property. Thus, a person having an equal right with applicants, is one who is entitled to grant in the same degree as the applicants. In other words, an equal right exists where a person to be served notice under this category has equal interest, claim or ownership with applicants in the estate of the deceased.

Instances where such notice is served in the Registry include:

1. Where the applicants to a grant sought are the children of the deceased, notice is served on the remaining adult children, if any[10]
2. Where the applicants are spouse of the deceased or a spouse and any of the children of the deceased, notice will be served on the remaining adult children other than the applicant.

It is pertinent to note that, in grant of Letters of Administration with Will Annexed, the grant may be made to any person entitled thereto without notice to other persons entitled in the same degree.(11)

REPLY TO NOTICE

The reply to notice served on person having equal right with applicants to the grant sought must be addressed to the Registrar and is expected to reach him within fourteen (14) days of service of the notice.

In practice however, the reply to notice is usually termed "Consent Letter" and is returned along with the second set of Probate forms. The Consent Letter can be submitted either personally by the persons served or on behalf of the persons served by the applicants to the grant sought. Where persons served reside together or live within the same jurisdiction, reply to notice collectively signed by them is acceptable.

AFFIDAVIT OF WITNESS/ATTESTATION

In line with the provision of order 58 Rule 12(2)[12], a reply to notice submitted by applicants to the grant sought on behalf of persons served is usually accompanied by an Affidavit of Witness or Attestation.

The affidavit is sworn to by one of the applicants who witnessed the signing of the consent by person served and if the consent is not witnessed by any of the applicants, one of the applicants must through an affidavit, attest to the fact that the consent emanated from the person served and the signature thereon. Affidavit of Witness or Attestation must be filed in the Registry.

However, where the consent is personally submitted by person served and signed in the presence of an authorized officer

[13] after due identification by the person served, this affidavit will be dispensed with.

NOTICE OF APPLICATION TO PERSON HAVING PRIOR RIGHT OVER APPLICANTS

A person is said to have a prior right if the person's interest, claim or ownership in the estate of the deceased is higher in degree or rank over that of applicant to the grant sought.

By virtue of the proviso to Order 58 Rule 10 of the High Court of Edo State (Civil Procedure) Rules, 2018, notice to person having a prior right over applicants is served on someone whose right to grant takes precedence over that of the applicants or one of them. The purpose of the notice is to inform such a person of his prior right to grant of Letters of Administration over the applicants to the grant sought. Usually attached to this notice is a Renunciation form.

Instances where this notice is served in the Registry include:

i. Where the applicants are children of the deceased, notice will be served on the surviving spouse of the deceased.

ii. Where one of the children of the deceased is a co-applicant with any of the following relation of the deceased:
   (a) Parent
   (b) Niece
   (c) Brother
   (d) Sister
   (e) Aunty
   (f) Nephew
   (g) Cousin
   (h) Grand Parent

(i) Grand Child etc

Notice is served on surviving spouse and other children of the deceased above eighteen (18) years, except the applicant.

iii. Where a spouse married under Native Law and Custom is a co-applicant with any of the above mentioned relation of the deceased, notice is served on children above eighteen (18) years and the surviving parent of the deceased, if any.

However, where a spouse is a co-applicant with the relation of the deceased and the children are minor (below eighteen (18) years) or a childless marriage, notice is served on surviving parent of the deceased. But where marriage contracted is under the law[14] and the Marriage Act Certificate is filed along with the first set of Probate forms and the children are all minor, notice will not be served on surviving parent of the deceased. Thus, the spouse is at liberty to co-administer with whomsoever. Though, where such marriage is childless, the spouse is under obligation to co-administer with a relative of the deceased only.

iv. Where the estate of an unmarried deceased person with no child or having minor children is to be administered by relation of the deceased other than the parents, notice is served on the surviving parent of the deceased. Also, where such a deceased's estate is to be administered by either of the parent and any relation, notice will be served on the other parent, if any.

v. Where the estate of a married deceased person with children above eighteen (18) years is to be administered by his/her relations, notice will be served on the surviving spouse and children of the deceased above eighteen (18) years.

RENUNCIATION OF APPLICATION

Renunciation in relation to Administration of estate means the act of waiving a right under a Will or Intestacy.[(15)] Where Notice of application is served on person having a prior right over the applicants to the grant sought, Renunciation form is attached and renunciation must be tacit.[(16)] Therefore a person having a prior right over the applicants must expressly waived such right to enable the applicants obtain the grant sought. And moreover, without the renunciation of persons with prior right, payment of estate fee is unacceptable. Renunciation can be done either at the Registry or Magistrate's Court. Renunciation does not disinherit the person renouncing of his share of the deceased's estate but only preclude such person from the Administration of the deceased's estate.

However, persons served with this Notice of application, have the option of exercising their right over the grant sought.

HOW TO RENOUNCE

Where a person served with a notice of prior right decides to waive such right over the grant sought, the Renunciation Form attached to the notice is filled by an officer of the court. After payment for Oath, the person renouncing is made to sign before the Commissioner for Oaths. The executed Renunciation Form must be filed at the Registry. It is vital to note that renunciation must be done in person and therefore, can be done in any State or Country Probate Registry, before an authorized officer, that is, any officer of a Registry who is for the time being, authorized by law to administer any oath or to take any affidavit required for any purpose connected with his duties.

INSTANCES WHERE BOTH CATEGORIES OF NOTICE OF APPLICATION ARE SERVED

i. Where a spouse co-administer with the children of a deceased who is survived by more than one wife, notice of application of a prior right will be served on the other wives, while notice of equal right will be served on other children above eighteen (18) years of age.

ii. Where there is a surviving spouse but children of the deceased are to administer the estate, notice of application of prior right will be served on the spouse and notice of application of equal right will be served on deceased children above eighteen (18) years of age other than the applicants.

REFERENCES

(1) "Notice" is the legal notification required by Law or agreement or imparted by the operation of Law as a result of some fact - see Garner, B. A., "Black's Law Dictionary", supra pg. 1164

(2) A Property Right means a right to specific property, whether tangible or intangible.

(3) See Garner, B. A., "Black's Law Dictionary", supra pg. 1257.

(4) Or.58 R.10 (Edo) 2018; Or.54 R.10 (Delta) 2009 and Or.57 R.9 (Lagos) 2012, supra.

(5) Other than the Applicants to the grant sought.

(6) When collecting second set of Probate forms.

(7) Signing on behalf of the Registrar.

(8) See Appendix 38 for specimen of Notice of Application to a person having "equal right" with Applicants.

(9) See Appendix 39 for specimen of Notice of Application to a person having "prior right" over Applicants.

(10) Deceased Children above Eighteen (18) years of age, except the Applicants.

(11) Or.59 R.44(1) (Edo) 2018; Or.55 R.44(1) (Delta) 2009 and Or.59 R.13 (Lagos) 2012, supra.

(12) High Court of Edo (Civil Procedure) Rules, 2018.

(13) Any officer of the Registry who is authorized to administer any Oath or to take any affidavit required for any purpose connected with his duties.

(14) A valid Registry Marriage.

(15) Garner, B. A., "Black's Law Dictionary", supra pg. 1412.

(16) See the Proviso to Or.58 R.10 (Edo) 2018.

CHAPTER NINE

GRANT

It is the duty of the Registrar to apply for and obtain an Order from the Honourable, the Chief Judge of the State before any grant can be issued.

PREPARATION OF GRANT: MINUTE AND ORDER

After the payment of estate fee and the final approval of Sureties [(1)] a formal request, known as Minute and Order[(2)], is then prepared, signed by the Registrar, addressed and presented before the Honourable, the Chief Judge of the State, in chambers: for an Order to issue Probate or letters of Administration to the proposed Executors or Administrators to the grant sought.

The Minute and Order are both attached to the front page of the estate file of the deceased. Once the signature of the Chief Judge is obtained on the Order for Grant, the Minute and Order are then recorded in the Order book and a copy of the Order is filed in the estate file. Thus, immediately the Order for Grant sought is granted and signed by the Chief Judge, the Probate or Letters of Administration is thereafter prepared and signed by the Registrar. As soon as the Registrar signed, the Grant is ready for collection and the Executors or Administrators are duly informed.

The Grant is always made in three (3) copies. The original is given to the Executors or Administrators, the duplicate is filed in the estate file and the triplicate is pasted in the Deed Register kept in the Registry. No Grant of Probate or Letters of Administration with Will Annexed is to be issued within seven (7) days of the death of the deceased and no grant of Letters of

Administration (Without Will) will be issued within fourteen days of such death.[3]

Persons to whom the grant of Probate or Letters of Administration is made cannot be more than four or less than two individuals. The period between the payment of Estate fee and collection of Grant is usually less than fourteen days.

CONTENT OF GRANT

A grant must contain the following:

i. The deceased's estate file number;
ii. The effective date of the grant;[4]
iii. The full names of the deceased;
iv. The native place of the deceased;[5]
v. The deceased's fixed place of abode;[6]
vi. The date and place of death;
vii. The names and addresses of the Executors or Administrators;
viii. The relationship between the deceased and the Executors or Administrators;
ix. The estate sworn to;[7]
x. The red seal and the seal of the Registry;
xi. The Registrar's signature.

Listed at the back of the grant are:

i. The amount of fees expected to be paid
ii. The purposes of such payment
iii. The receipt numbers issued for payment
iv. The total sum of amount paid

AMENDMENT AND REVOCATION OF GRANT

No grant is to be amended or revoked, except in special circumstances, upon the application or with the consent of the person to whom the grant was made.(8)

Amendment of grant involves minor alteration which does not affect the validity of the grant. It can be due to typographical errors, omissions etc Amendment must be fixable and tenable. It is usually done upon the application or with the consent of the persons to whom the grant was made.

Revocation of grant simply means the cancellation or invalidation of a grant by the Registrar due to special circumstances. Thus, obtaining grant by fraud or misrepresentation may be special circumstances for the revocation of such grant. Once the Registrar is satisfied that a grant should be amended or revoked, such an Order is complied with accordingly.(9)

GROUNDS FOR REVOCATION OF GRANT

The following are some of the grounds upon which a grant can be revoked:

i. Where a grant has been issued in respect of the estate of a person presumed dead but who thereafter is discovered to be alive.

ii. Where a grant has been obtained by fraud or issued to an Executor of an invalid, revoked or forged Will.

iii. Where a grant has been issued to the Administrator-General public trustee, but the next–of–kin of the deceased who are interested in the Administration of the deceased's estate are later discovered.

iv. Where a person whom a grant has been issued, has no sufficient title to the grant or the grant is issued to a wrong person or to an elected guardian of infants without clearing off those with prior right to the grant or is issued to a person falsely claiming to be the next-of-kin of the deceased.

v. The discovering of a later Will or Codicil altering or revoking appointment of the Executors named in the former Will after Probate of the former Will has been granted.

vi. The discovering of a will after the issuance of grant of Letters of Administration (without Will).(10)

WAYS OF REVOKING GRANT

A grant can be revoked in any of the following ways:

THROUGH THE REGISTRY

No grant may be revoked except on the application of or with the consent of the person to whom the grant was issued. Thus, if such person consent to the revocation and the Registrar is satisfied that there are sufficient grounds for the revocation, the affected grant shall be revoked accordingly.(11)

THROUGH THE COURT BY SUMMONS

Where the person to whom the grant was issued does not consent to revocation, but he is not affected by the revocation, application for revocation of the grant under this circumstance may be made to the Court by Originating Summons or by a Motion, with the Registrar and the person to whom the grant was issued as necessary parties.

Thus, a certified true copy of the Order of Court revoking the grant must be obtained and filed in the Registry for the Registrar's compliance accordingly.

It is important to note that Originating Summons should only be applicable in circumstances where there is no dispute on question of fact or likelihood of such dispute and it should not be a substitute for initiating contentious issues of fact.

BY WAY OF A WRIT OF SUMMONS

A writ of Summons is appropriate where there is likelihood of substantial dispute of fact. Thus, where the issuance of grant is challenged and the person to whom the grant was made does not consent to its revocation and he is unwilling to be discharged or removed as personal representative of the deceased, revocation of the grant can be obtained by commencement of a Probate Court Action with a Writ of Summons. [12]

TRANSFER OF GRANT

Any Executor or Administrator may, with the consent of the Administrator –General, transfer the assets of the estate vested in him by virtue of a grant of Probate or Letters of Administration to the Administrator-General.

Thus:

"(1) Any private executor or administrator may, with the previous consent of the Administrator-General by instrument in writing under his hand, notified in the State Gazette, transfer the asset vested in him by virtue of a grant of probate or letters of administration to the Administrator-General by that name.

(2) As from the date of such transfer, the transferor shall be exempt from all liability as such executor or administrator, as the case may be except in respect of acts or omission done or committed before the date of such transfer."[13]

REFERENCES

(1) In respect of Letters of Administration.

(2) See Appendix 36, 37 &43for specimen of Minute and Order.

(3) Or.58 R.1(3) & Or.59 R.9(3)(Edo State) 2018.

(4) That is, the date the Order was signed by the Chief Judge.

(5) The deceased's village, Local Government and State of Origin (other than Edo State).

(6) Must be within the jurisdiction of the High Court of Edo State.

(7) The estate of the deceased covered by the grant; for example: Money in Bank, Shares, Pension, Gratuity, Landed Properties, etc.

(8) Or.59 R.56 (Edo) 2018; Or.55 R.56 (Delta) 2009; Or.57 R.19 (Lagos) 2012 and section 20 AEL (Bendel) 1976, supra.

(9) Ibid. How power to administer estate is vested and revoked: see the case of Bakare V. Bakare (2012) 16 NWLR (pt.1325) p.29.

(10) See section 11 AEL (Bendel) 1976.

(11) Or.59 R.56 (Edo) 2018; Or.55 R.56 (Delta) 2009; Or.57 R.19 (Lagos) 2012 and section 20 AEL (Bendel) 1976.

(12) See Mosanya, J. A., "Common Form Probate Business" supra pgs.186-191

(13) Section 32 AEL (Bendel) 1976, supra.

CHAPTER TEN

MEAGRE SUM ESTATE (SMALL ESTATE)

A deceased's estate can be classified as a Meagre Sum Estate (Small Estate) where the gross value of the estate, especially, money in the deceased's bank account which the personal representative seek to administer is less than or not more than ₦50,000.00 (fifty thousand naira).

According to Probate Rules, no grant of Letters of Administration can be issued in an estate which total value is less than or not more than ₦50,000.00 (fifty thousand naira). Instead, a Meagre Sum Letter is issued in place of a grant of Letters of Administration.

Therefore, applicants or personal representative seeking grant of Letters of Administration to administer a deceased's money in bank which is less than or not more than ₦50,000.00 (fifty thousand naira) must apply to the Registrar for a Meagre Sum Letter. It is important to note that the said letter cannot be used to administer shares, even if the value of such shares is less that ₦50,000.00 (fifty thousand naira).

MEAGRE SUM APPLICATION

A Meagre Sum Application is a formal request from a deceased's personal representative who seek to administer a Meagre Sum balance in the deceased's bank account.

This application is very necessary once the bank certificate issued to the personal representative to obtain deceased's account balance shows an amount less than or not more than ₦50,000.00 (fifty thousand naira) and this money happens to be the only estate of the deceased which the personal representative seek to administer. The said amount can be a total sum from more than one bank. Thus, a deceased's personal representative can apply for more than one meagre sum letter at the same time, provided the total sum of the amount in the deceased's different bank accounts does not exceed ₦50,000.00 (Fifty Thousand Naira).

The application is addressed to the Registrar, appealing to him to enable them claim the said Meagre Sum balance by causing a letter to be written to the Bank Manager of the branch where the deceased's money was deposited, to release same to them. Two copies of the application are usually submitted. One is to be filed in the deceased's estate file while the other must be attached to the Meagre Sum Letter addressed to the Bank Manager.

PROCEDURE FOR MEAGRE SUM LETTER

Upon the Bank Certificate issued together with the other first set of Probate forms to personal representative or applicants for Letters of Administration (Without Will) shows money in deceased's bank account which is less than or not more than N50,000.00 (fifty thousand naira) and this form the only estate which the applicants seek to administer, such applicants are advised by the interviewing officer to apply for Meagre Sum Letter.(1)

After the interview, applicants are made to pay for Oath and filing only. Immediately after the oath has been administered, a file is opened in respect of the deceased's estate matter and the Meagre Sum Application which must be typed, addressed to the Registrar and signed by all the applicants is then forwarded for approval.

Once the application is approved, a Meagre Sum Letter signed by the Registrar and addressed to the Bank Manager of the branch in which the deceased's account was opened, is issued to applicants, requesting the Bank Manager to release the said amount accordingly. Attached to this Meagre Sum Letter, is a copy of applicants' Meagre Sum Application.

CONTENT OF MEAGRE SUM LETTER

A Meagre Sum Letter is like a Court Order,[(2)] requesting Bank Manager to pay the persons whose names are written in the letter, the balance of money in a deceased's bank account in line with the Meagre Sum Application appeal attached thereto and since the amount involved is meagre, it does not attracts stringent requirements for Letters of Administration. The letter is accordingly complied with by Bank Managers.

The basic content of the letter include:

i. The deceased's estate file number and date
ii. The bank branch manager whom the letter is addressed to
iii. The deceased's full names
iv. The names of the deceased's personal representative
v. The relationship between the deceased and the personal representative
vi. The deceased's account balance
vii. The deceased's account number
viii. The signature of the Registrar.

It is important to know that in Meagre Sum estate, applicants are exempted from paying Estate fee, only filing and oath fees are paid.[(3)]

REFERENCES

(1) See Appendix 31 for a specimen of Letter for Meagre Sum.

(2) Court Order is a written direction or command delivered by a Court or Judge - see Garner, B. A., "Black's Law Dictionary", supra pg.1205.

(3) See Second Schedule paragraph 21 High Court of Edo State (Civil Procedure) Rules, 2018.

CHAPTER ELEVEN

FINANCIAL ASSISTANCE

Financial Assistance is an assistance made available to a deceased's personal representative who have commenced the process of obtaining grant but are having the challenges of raising fund for the estate fee due to circumstances beyond their control and the deceased in question happens to have more than sufficient amount of money in his bank account that could be used to pay the estate fee chargeable on the deceased's estate. Such deceased's personal representative can solicit the assistance of the Registrar to enable them withdraw the said amount chargeable as estate fee on the deceased's estate from the deceased's account with the said bank which has a balance that is more than sufficient to settle the estate fee.

PROCEDURE FOR FINANCIAL ASSISTANCE

The solicitation by the personal representative for the deduction of estate fee from the deceased's bank account, can be done through an application for Financial Assistance in respect of a deceased's estate. The application must be typed, addressed to the Registrar and signed by all the applicants or one of them, with the consent of the co-applicant. Where the estate of the deceased is legally represented, the application can be signed by the legal practitioner representing the deceased's estate.

Once the application is approved, the Registrar would cause a letter to be written and addressed to the Bank Manager of the branch where the deceased opened the account.[(1)]This letter is issued to the personal representative for onward delivery to the Bank Manager of the deceased's bank.

Financial Assistance is usually complied with by Bank Managers. However, in Probate Registry, High Court of Edo State, this assistance is not available where deceased's fund is with Pension Managers, but money in banks only. Immediately after the bank's verification of the letter, a Bank Draft is issued in favour of the Registrar for the amount chargeable as estate fee.

It is important to note that this assistance can be solicited from more than one bank. For example, where the deceased had various accounts and the balance in one account is not more than sufficient to settle the estate fee chargeable, however, deduction from two accounts can off-set the estate fee, then financial assistance will be solicited from both accounts. These accounts can be from the same bank or from different banks.

This assistance is equally made available to deceased's personal representative who are able to raised part of the estate fee on their own and only wish to solicit for the other part from the deceased's account balance.

REFERENCE

(1) See Appendix 30 for a specimen of Letter for Financial Assistance.

CHAPTER TWELVE

WILLS

A Will can be defined as the legal expression of an individual's wishes about the disposition of his or her property after death; especially a document by which a person directs his or her estate to be distributed upon death.[1] Generally, a Will is a testamentary and revocable document, voluntarily made, executed and witnessed according to law by a Testator with sound disposing mind wherein he disposes of his property subject to any limitation imposed by Law and wherein he gives such other directives as he may deem fit to his personal representatives otherwise known as his Executors, who administer his estate in accordance with the wishes manifested in the Will.[2]

A Will can also be called Testament or Testamentary instrument. The phrase "Last Will and Testament" is deemed to be the most recent Will of the deceased or instrument ultimately fixing the disposition of real and personal property at the Testator's death. All property may be disposed of by Will, subject to any Customary Law relating thereto.[3]

Wills and Will-making is an arrangement that ensures that the property of a person devolved on his heirs according to his express wishes and directives after death. This makes a Will very important as it is a document that speaks after the death of the Testator.[4] By virtue of Section 3 Wills Law of Edo State, a Will may deal not only with the real property but also with personal and moveable properties.

Any person of full legal age and the right mental capacity can make a Will without undue influence. Under the Wills Law of Edo State, no Will made by any person under the age of twenty-one (21) years shall be valid.[5]

ADVANTAGES OF MAKING A WILL

The following are some of the Advantages of making a valid Will as against not making will:[(6)]

i. A Testator may in his lifetime appoint personal representatives (Executors) of his choice. The Testator may confer on his Executor the powers of a Trustee. But where he died Intestate, Probate may be granted to Administrators to administer the estate of the deceased. These Administrators may be persons not desired by the Testator.

ii. A Testator may by his Will show affection to those he loves, reward the loyalty of others who have served him well. He may as well as make a gift to charity or persons that are not related to him by blood or otherwise. But where he died Intestate, only persons related to him can benefit from his estate

iii. A Testator may by his Will appoint a guardian for his infant dependant. If this is done, the Law will give effect to such appointment or nomination.

iv. Each State of the Federation has in operation an Administration of Estate Law which prescribes rules on succession to real and personal estate in the case of Intestacy.[(7)]

   Thus, a Testator may by his Will displace the prescribed rules of inheritance and state specifically who he wants to benefit.

v. All tribes in Nigeria have Customary Laws and Rules governing who takes what in the estate of a deceased person who died Intestate. Except a deceased left a Will, his estate could devolve to people outside his contemplation.

Thus, subject to the rule of Custom, a Testator may under his Will disinherit any person according to his desires.

vi. A Testator might in his lifetime give instruction of where he should be buried and the form of burial rites to be given to him.

Usually, a Will is read after the funeral ceremonies are over. It is submitted that Testator should be advised to inform his Executors in a separate documents about his burial arrangements, so that his wish could be carried out pending when the Will is read.

vii. Where the deceased person died Testate; there is continuity in the Administration of his estate. By the Operation of Law, the Executor of the Last Surviving Executor shall continue to administer his estate.(8)

viii. It is cheaper to obtain grant of Probate (if the deceased died Testate) than to obtain grant of Letters of Administration (if the deceased died Intestate). This is as a result of the involvement of Bond and the production of Sureties in the process of obtaining grant of Letters of Administration. Since the Testator chooses his personal representative in his Will, the Court therefore dispenses with Bond and the production of Sureties.

CONTENT OF A WILL

Although there is no specific format by the Operation of Law as to the content of a Will, however in practice, the following are considered as a uniform order of arrangement of clauses in a Will (9):

COMMENCEMENT CLAUSE

This is also known as Introductory Clause; Exordium Clause. It include full names of the Testator, address, occupation and the date of the Will.

REVOCATION CLAUSE

Revocation Clause is usually inserted in every Will, revoking all former testamentary dispositions made by the Testator, if any.

APPOINTMENT OF EXECUTORS AND TRUSTEES CLAUSE

An Executor is a person appointed by the Testator and vested with the power to carry out the Testator's wishes in accordance with the Will. Persons appointed as Executor are usually instructed to act as Trustees. By the Operation of Law the number of Executors appointed should not be more than four.

CHARGING CLAUSE

This clause is actually for the benefit of professional executors permitted to charge professional fees, such as a solicitor acting as individual or by his firm.

LEGACIES CLAUSE

Legacy is also termed Bequest; Devise and it simply means a gift by Will. This clause provides for the various gifts the Testator wishes to distribute among his beneficiaries.

RESIDUARY CLAUSE

This is a testamentary clause that disposes of any estate property remaining after the satisfaction of all other gifts. This clause take care of the left over estate property after the part of the estate given to the beneficiaries under the Will has been disposed of.

MISCELLANEOUS CLAUSE

This clause is of great importance as it may serve as a means of expressing other intentions of the Testator, for instance, conferring special powers on the Executors/Trustees.

TESTIMONIUM CLAUSE

It is also known as Testatum Clause; Witness Clause and it is the provision at the end of a Will, reciting the date when the Will was signed, by whom it was signed and in what capacity.

EXECUTION AND ATTESTATION CLAUSE

This must be done according to Law. In other words, it must recite the formalities required by the jurisdiction where the Will might be probated.

LODGEMENT OF WILL

According to Law, once a Will is executed, there is need for it to be lodged or deposited at the Registry.(10)

Therefore:

> *"Any person may, in his lifetime, deposit for safe custody in the Court at Benin City, his own Will, sealed up under his own seal and the seal of the Court."* (11)

Also, it is a statutory duty of a person having in his possession any paper or writing of any person deceased, being or purporting to be testamentary (12) to deliver same to the Registrar within fourteen (14) days after having had knowledge of the death of such person and failure to do so, attracts a fine not exceeding ₦50,000.00 (fifty thousand naira)[13]

Thus, a Will can be lodged before or immediately after the Testator's death. Where a Will is to be lodged after the death of the Testator, the person in possession of such Will must satisfy the Registrar why the Will was not deposited during the Testator's lifetime.[14] Thereafter, the Will can be lodged and read.

A Will can be deposited by the Testator himself. Although, in practice, it is usually the Lawyer who drafted the Will who deposits the Will on behalf of his client. There is no law that prohibit non- lawyers from drafting a Will, but it is better that the Testator should consult a Lawyer. All Wills to be lodged are put in sealed envelopes. The envelope must bear the following:

i. The full names and address of the Testator and the date the Will was made.
ii. The names and addresses of the executors and they must be described as such.[15]
iii. The signature, name and address of the Legal Practitioner who drafted the Will.[16]

The envelope containing the Will must be presented before an officer of the Registry who inspect the envelope and ensure that it states the Testator's full names, address and is sealed and waxed. If the officer is satisfied that the format complies with the requirements of the Registry, the office initials the Will and the depositor [17] takes it to the cashier and pays the prescribed fee. The Will is then entered into the Will Register. The entering in the Will register comprises:

i. The lodgment date
ii. The receipt number

iii. The name and address of Testator
iv. The name and address of depositor
v. Will number
vi. Signature of receiver[18]

Thereafter, the envelope containing the Will is sealed and stamped with the Registry seal and stamp and the Will's number is written on it before taken into safe custody. After a Will have been deposited, it may not be delivered to the Testator or any other person, unless in special circumstances the Registrar so directs.[19]

WITHDRAWAL AND REVOCATION OF WILL

Any person who wishes to withdraw or revoke his deposited Will in the Registry is entitled to do so.

A Will is a testamentary document of a living person that becomes effective once the person is dead. In other words, a will speaks from the death of the testator.[20]Therefore until the death of a Testator, a Will is a mere declaration of his intention and the Testator is free during his lifetime, as many times over as he wishes to withdraw, alter, amend and even revoke it.

PROCEDURE FOR WITHDRAWAL OF WILL

Withdrawal of Will is the act of taking back a Will already deposited in the Registry by a Testator or his legal representative. Thus, a Testator who has his Will deposited in the Registry can apply to the Registrar for the withdrawal of such Will. The application can be made personally or through the legal representative of the Testator's estate. Attached to such application is the lodgment receipt issued to the depositor the day the said Will was lodged. In the absence of lodgment receipt due to loss, a sworn affidavit to that effect may suffice.

Immediately the Registrar approves the application and the prescribed fee having been paid, the column on the Will Register where the Will was recorded on the day of lodgment is endorsed to reflect the withdrawal and the person withdrawing the Will is made to write his name, signature and date on that same column, after which the Will is handed over.

In most cases where a Testator intends to withdraw a deposited Will, there is lodgment of a replacement Will immediately before or after the withdrawal.

REVOCATION OF WILL

Revocation of Will means the invalidation of a Will by the Testator, either by destroying the Will or by executing a new one.(21)

There are various ways by which a Will may be revoked(22) but the most popular ones in the Registry are:

i. By a subsequent Will or codicil
ii. By an instrument in writing

REVOCATION BY A SUBSEQUENT WILL OR CODICIL

A subsequent Will or codicil can expressly revoke an earlier Will with the insertion of an appropriate "revocation clause" in the later Will.(23)

However, even without an express revocation clause, a later Will can revoke an earlier one if the later Will covers practically the same ground as the earlier one. In this case, it is implied that the later one takes the place of the earlier Will and Probate will be granted to the later Will. Thus, another Will or codicil may expressly or impliedly revoke an earlier Will.

REVOCATION BY AN INSTRUMENT IN WRITING

A Will can also be revoked by an instrument in writing, expressing the Testator's intention to revoke earlier testamentary instruments deposited in the registry.(24)

For such writing to be valid as an instrument of revocation, it must comply with all the requirements for making a valid Will and must be addressed to the Registrar. The envelope containing any of such Instrument must indicate that it is meant to revoke a Will or Codicil bearing a particular date, Will or Codicil number and lodgment date. This envelope is classified and filed with the Will or Codicil it purports to revoke and the entry in the Will register is endorsed to reflect the revocation.

NOTIFICATION OF TESTATOR'S DEATH AND APPLICATION FOR READING OF WILL

By Law, the Registrar is the custodian of all Wills lodged or deposited in the Registry and upon the death of a Testator, the personal or legal representative of the Testator's estate, must through a letter notify the Registrar of the Testator's death.

In practice, this Notification usually contains a request for the reading of such Testator's Will. Thus, suggested dates are stated in the Notification/Application letter. Attached to such letter are:

i. The original or certified true copy of the medical certificate of death or a certificate of proof of death issued by the Local Government Council of the area where the Testator lived before his death.

ii. A copy of the lodgment receipt (25)

INVITATION IN RESPECT OF READING OF WILL

As soon as the application for reading of Will is approved by the Registrar, a date is set aside, usually from the suggested dates stated in the application for reading of Will and invitation letter in respect of the reading of such Will is sent, inviting the executors, children, family members and close relatives of the Testator, to come to the Registry on the said date and time, to witness the opening and reading of the Testator's Will.[(26)]

OPENING AND READING OF WILL

On the appointed day for the reading of Will, a Register of interested persons who have come to witness the opening and reading of the Will is opened. These persons must register their names, addresses, relationship to the Testator and also sign in the Register. After the registration of interested persons present, they are taken to the Wills' room.[(27)]At the Wills' room, the attendance list of registered persons is called and thereafter the sealed envelope containing the Testator's Will is presented by the Registrar and shown to all present to ensure that it has not been previously tampered with or opened. Then, the Will is opened and read by the Registrar.

Immediately after the reading of a Will, copies of such Will are made available; certified true copy can be applied for and obtain by persons interested or the legal representative of the Testator's estate, on payment of the prescribed fee.

REFERENCES

(1) Garner, B. A., " Black's Law Dictionary", supra pg.1735.

(2) Abayomi, K., "Wills: Law and Practice", Mbeyi & Associates (Nig.) Ltd, Lagos (2004) pg.6.

(3) See section 3(1) Wills Law Cap. 172 Vol. Vi Laws of Defunct Bendel State of Nigeria 1976 as applicable in Edo State. See the following cases: Idehen V. Idehen (1991) 6 NWLR (pt.198) p.382; Agidigbi V. Agidigbi (1992) 2 NWLR (pt.224) p.98; Lawal Osula V. Lawal Osula (1992) 2 NWLR (pt.221) p.98; Egharevba V. Okunghae (2001) 11 NWLR (pt.724) p.336 and Igbinosun & Ors V. 0ka & Ors (2002) 2 Edo HCLR p.332. See also Otoghile, J.O., " The Place of a Will in relation to Igiogbe Inheritance", A Seminar Paper Presented As A Ph.D. Student in the Faculty of Law, Ambrose Alli University Ekpoma, Edo State, 2016.

(4) See sections 21 & 3(1) Wills Law, supra. Also see the case of 0kelola V. Boyle (1998) 2 NWLR (pt.539) p.533. Thus until the Testator's death, the Will is only a mere declaration of his intention.

(5) Section 5 Wills Law, supra.

(6) For detailed study of the advantages of making a Will, see Imhanobe, S. O.,: "Legal Drafting And Conveyancing", (2nd Edition), Sylvester Imhanobe Legal Research Ltd, Abuja, 2007, pgs 413-415; Abayomi, K. "Wills: Law And Practice", Mbeyi & Associates (Nig.) Ltd, 2004 pgs 8-12.

(7) See section 49 AEL (Bendel) 1976, supra

(8) Section 8, ibid

(9) See Imhanobe, S. O.,: "Legal Drafting And Conveyancing", supra, pgs. 473-476.

(10) Presented to an authority, that is, the Registrar for proper safe keeping and Custody.

(11) Or.58 R.16 & Or.59 R. 28 (Edo) 2018; Or.54 R.16 & Or. 55 R.28 (Delta) 2009 and Or.58 R.1 (Lagos) 2012, supra.

(12) The Original of the Will or Testament.

(13) Or.58 R.4 & Or.59 R.1 (Edo) 2018; Or.54 R.4 & Or.55 R.1 (Delta) 2009 and Or.58 R.15 (Lagos) 2012, supra. NOTE: Under the Lagos Rules, such document must be delivered to the Registrar within Three (3) Months.

(14) Usually by an affidavit sworn to by such person.

(15) They should not be more than four. See section 24 AEL (Bendel) 1976, supra.

(16) On the reserved side of the envelope.

(17) Whoever that is depositing the Will.

(18) That is, the Cashier who receive the Will.

(19) Or.59 R.8(4) (Edo) 2018; Or.55 R.8(4) (Delta) 2009 and Or.57 R.3(4) (Lagos) 2012.

(20) See sections 21 & 3(1) Wills Law and also the case of Okeola V. Boyle (1998), supra.

(21) Garner, B.A., "Black's Law Dictionary", supra pg. 1435. See also section 17 Wills Law, supra.

(22) A Will or parts of a Will, may be revoked by the operation of Law. See section 15 Wills Law, supra.

(23) See section 17 Wills Law, supra.

(24) Ibid. See also Abayomi, K. "Wills: Law and Practice" supra, pg. 181.

(25) The receipt issued to the depositor the day the Will was deposited.

(26) See Appendix 34 for specimen of Letter of invitation for reading of Will.

(27) Where the Will is usually read.

CHAPTER THIRTEEN

ADMITTING WILL TO PROOF

Probate simply means the judicial procedure by which a testamentary document is established to be a valid Will or the proving of a Will to the satisfaction of the court.(1) It can also be defined as admitting will to proof.

EXAMINATION OF WILL

After the reading of a Will and upon application for Probate(2) by the Executors named in the Will or the legal representative of the Testator's estate, the Will must be examined by the Registrar, as to its due execution and compliance with the Wills Law and other related Enactments. There are essential requirements that every Will must comply with to qualify as a valid Will. No Will shall be valid unless:

i. It must be voluntarily made;
ii. The testator must have a sound mind;
iii. It must name the beneficiary;
iv. It must be attested and subscribed to by two credible witnesses;
v. It must identify the property.

The formal requirements for the execution of a Will according to the wills Law are as follows:

i. It must be in writing;
ii. It must be signed by the testator or signed by some other person in his presence and at his direction;
iii. The testator must make and acknowledge his signature in the presence of at least two witnesses;

iv. The witnesses must attest and subscribe to the will in the presence of the testator but no form of attestation shall be necessary.[3]

Every adult person whether he is a Christian, Muslim or otherwise may make Will. The age of adulthood is a matter of law provided in the Wills Law applicable to the Testator's place of domicile.

Thus

"No Will made by any person under the age of twenty-one years shall be valid."[4]

Examination of Will before admitting it to proof is to establish that the Will was duly executed and satisfied the requirement of a valid Will. Therefore, according to the provisions of the following rules:

A"(1) *On receiving an application for probate or for administration with Will annexed, the Court shall inspect the Will, and see whether it appears to be signed by the testator, or by some other person in his presence, and by his direction, and to be subscribed by two witnesses according to the enactments relative thereto, and shall not proceed further if the Will does not appear to be so signed and subscribed.*

(2) If the Will appears to be so signed and subscribed, the Court shall then refer to the attestation clause (if any), and consider whether the wording thereof states the Will to have been, in fact, executed in accordance with those enactments."[5]

B"(1) *The Court, on being satisfied that the Will was duly executed, shall carefully inspect it to see whether there are any interlineations or alterations, or erasures, if obliterations appearing in it and requiring to be accounted for."*[(6)]

It is of practical importance to note the following:

i. Interlineations, alterations erasures and obliterations are invalid[(7)] unless they existed in the Will at the time of its execution or if made afterwards, they have been executed and attested in the mode required by relevant enactments or they have been made invalid by the re-execution[(8)] of the Will or by the subsequent execution of a Codicil.[(9)]

ii. Where interlineations, alterations, erasures or obliterations appear in the Will an affidavit in proof of their having existed, in the Will before its execution, must be filed.[(10)]

iii. Where no satisfactory evidence is adduced in respect of the time when an erasure or obliteration was made and the words erased or obliterated are not entirely defected and can, on inspection of the Will, be ascertained, they shall form part of the Probate.[(11)]

iv. Where any words have been erased which might have been of importance, an affidavit must be required.[(12)]

v. Where there appears in a Will any obliteration, interlineations or other alteration which is not authenticated in the manner prescribed by law or by the re-execution of the Will or by the execution of a Codicil, the Registrar must require evidence to show whether the alteration was present at the time the Will was executed and shall give directions as to the form in which the Will is to be proved.(13)

vi. Where a Will contains alternations which are not admissible to proof, an engrossment of the Will must be lodged in the form which the Will is to be proved. Any engrossment lodged must reproduce the punctuation, spacing and division into paragraphs of the Will.(14)

vii. If from the examination of a Will, any mark appears to the Registrar that some other documents has been attached to the Will or if a Will contains any reference to another document in such terms as to suggest that it ought to be incorporated in the Will, the Registrar may require the document to be produced and may call for such evidence in regards to the attaching or incorporation of the document as he deem fit.(15}
Nevertheless, a document cannot form part of a Will unless it was in existence at the time the Will was executed.

viii. Any appearance of attempted revocation of a Will by burning, tearing or otherwise, observed during the examination of a Will and every other circumstance leading to a presumption of revocation by the testator must be accounted for, to the satisfaction of the Registrar.(16)

C *"Before admitting to proof, a Will which appears to have been signed by a blind or illiterate testator or by another person by direction of the testator, or which for any other reason gives rise to doubt as to the testator having had knowledge of the contents of the Will at the time of its execution, the Registrar shall satisfy himself that the testator had such knowledge."*[17]

D *"if it appears to the Registrar that there is prima facie evidence that a Will is one to which section 9 of the Wills Act, 1837, or any provision of the equivalent enactment in force in the state applies, the Will may be admitted to proof, if the Registrar is satisfied that it was made by the testator in accordance with the provisions of that section or enactment, as the case may be."*[18]

The Examination of Will as to its due execution is very crucial in determining whether or not a grant of Probate or Letters of Administration with the Will Annexed can be issued. The due execution of a Will is as important as the testamentary capacity of the Testator. Where it is established that the Will was not executed according to Law, the Will is not valid and Probate is refused. The purpose of attestation is to prevent fraud. Therefore a Will is not admitted to Probate unless the names of the attesting witnesses are subscribed on it. No form of attestation is necessary but it is ideal to execute the Will in a form to show that the requirements of the Law are complied with. Ideally the signature of the witnesses should appear on the same page as that of the Testator.[19]

Therefore, if after the Examination of a Will, the Registrar is satisfied that all the requirements for a valid Will were complied with, application for Probate can then be proceeded with. In no case will the Court issue Probate or Letters of Administration with the Will Annexed until all inquiries which the Registrar deems fit to institute have been answered to his satisfaction.[20]By the operation of Law, the consequences of death without a will are the same as when a Will is invalid.

REFERENCES

(1) Garner, B.A., "Black's Law Dictionary", supra pg. 1321. See also section 2(1) AEL and the case of Nsefik V. Muna (2014), supra.
(2) That is, proving of the Will.
(3) Section 6 Wills Law and also see the case of Mudashiru V. Abdullahi (2011),supra.
(4) Section 5, ibid. NOTE: By the provisions of section 9, soldiers, airmen and mariners under the age of twenty-one(21) years are permitted to make Wills.
(5) Or.59 R. 31 & Or.58 R.19 (Edo) 2018; Or.55 R.19 & Or.54 R.19 (Delta) 2009 and Or.58 R.4 (Lagos) 2012, supra.
(6) Or.58 R.24(1) & Or,59 R.36 (Edo) 2018; Or.54 R.24(1) & Or.55 R.36 (Delta) and Or.58 R.11(1) (Lagos) 2012, supra.
(7) Of no practical importance.
(8) Re-execution is the equitable remedy by which a lost or destroyed deed or other instrument is replaced- Garner, B. A., "Black's Law Dictionary", supra, pg. 1393
(9) Or.58 R.24(2) (Edo) 2018; Or.54 R.24(2) (Delta) 2009 and Or.58 R.11(2) (Lagos), supra. See also section 18 Wills Law and the case of Mudashiru V. Abdullahi (2011), supra.
(10) Unless they are duly executed or recited in or otherwise identified by the attestation clause--Or.58 R.24(3)ibid; Or.54 R.24(3) ibid and Or.58 R.11(3) ibid
(11) Or.58 R.24(4) ibid; Or.54 R.24(4)ibid and Or.58 R.11(4) ibid.
(12) Or.58 R.24(5) ibid; Or.54 R.24(5) ibid and Or.58 R.11(4) ibid.

(13) This sub-rule does not apply to any alteration which appear to the Registrar to be of no practical importance- see Or.59 R16(1) (Edo) 2018; Or.55 R.16(1) (Delta) 2009 and Or.58 R.7(1) (Lagos) 2012, supra.

(14) Or.59 R.13(2)(3) (Edo) 2018; Or.55 R.13(2)(3) (Delta) 2009 and Or.58 R.20(2)(3) (Lagos) 2012, supra. NOTE: Engrossment means the preparation of a legal document (such as a deed) for execution.

(15) Or.59 R.16(2) , R.37 & Or.58 R.25 (Edo) 2018; Or.55 R.16(2) ,R.37 & Or. 54 R.25 (Delta) 2009 and Or.58 R.12 (Lagos) 2012, supra.

(16) Or.59 R.17 (Edo) 2018; Or.55 R.17 (Delta) 2009 and Or.58 R.8 (Lagos) 2012, supra.

(17) Or.59 R.15, R.35 & Or.58 R.23 (Edo) 2018; Or.55 R15,R.35 & Or.54 R.23 (Delta) 2009 and Or.58 R. 10 (Lagos) 2012, supra.

(18) Or.59 R.19 (Edo) 2018; Or.55 R.19 (Delta) 2009. NOTE: The provisions of section 9 Wills Law, supra is similar to section 9 of the Wills Act 1837. It deals with Wills of soldiers, airmen and mariners.

(19) See also the case of Mudashiru V. Abdullahi (2011), supra.

(20) Or.59 R.24 (Edo) 2018; Or.55 R.24 (Delta) 2009 and Or.59 R.6 (Lagos) 2012, supra.

CHAPTER FOURTEEN

IMPERFECT EXECUTION OF WILLS

Wills not fully in compliance with the Wills Law and other related Enactments cannot be admitted to proof, except the irregularities observed in the examination of such Wills are such that can be perfected.(1)

Thus:

> *"The Registrar may require an affidavit from any person he may think fit, for the purpose of satisfying himself as to any of the matters referred to in rules 15, 16 and 17* (2) *and in any such affidavit sworn by an attesting witness or other person present at the time of the execution of a Will, the deponent shall depose to the manner in which the Will was executed."*(3)

The due execution of a Will is as important as the testamentary capacity of the Testator. Where it is established that the Will was not executed according to Law, the Will is not valid and Probate is refused. Therefore, if on perusal of the affidavit, it appears that the Will was not in fact, executed in accordance with relevant enactments, the Registrar shall refuse Probate.(4)It is germane to buttress the fact that the consequences of death without a Will are the same as when the Will is invalid.

Therefore:

> *"If the Registrar, after considering the evidence:*
>
> *(a) Is satisfied that the Will was not duly executed he shall refuse probate and shall mark the Will accordingly.*
>
> *(b) Is doubtful whether the Will was duly executed, he may refer the matter to the Court on motion."*(5)

INSTANCES OF IMPERFECT EXECUTION OF WILLS

Some of the instances where Wills are said not to be properly executed include the following:

i. Where a Will is not signed by the Testator: if upon the examination of a Will, it appears not to be signed and subscribed by two (2) witnesses, the application for probate or administration with the Will annexed will not proceed further.(6)

ii. Where there is no attestation clause or the attestation clause is insufficient: Attestation clause is a provision at the end of the Will that is signed by the subscribing witnesses and that recites the formalities required by the jurisdiction in which the instrument might take effect (such as where the Will might be probated). The attestation strengthens the presumption that all the statutory requirements for executing the Will have been satisfied.(7)

Thus:

"(1) *Where a Will contains no attestation clause or the attestation clause is insufficient or where it appears to the Registrar that there is some doubt about the due execution of the Will, he shall before admitting it to proof, require an affidavit as to due execution from one or more of the attesting witnesses or, if no attesting witness is conveniently available, from any other person who was present at the time the Will was executed.*

(2) *If no affidavit can be obtained in accordance with the last foregoing*

paragraph, the Registrar may, if he thinks fit, having regard to the desirability of protecting the interest of any person who may be prejudiced by the Will, accept evidence on affidavit from any person he may think fit, to show that the signature on the Will is the handwriting of the deceased, or of any other matter which may raise a presumption in favour of the due execution of the Will."(8)

It is of practical importance to note that this affidavit must be engrossed and form part of the Probate so that the Probate may be a complete document on the face of it. (9)

iii. Where the state of the Will is such as to suggest it has been interfered with.

Therefore;

"If there are vestiges of sealing wax or wafers, or other marks on the Will, leading to the inference that some documents have been at sometime annexed or attached thereto, a satisfactory account of them shall be proved or the production of the document shall be required, and if it is not produced, a satisfactory account of its non-production shall be proved."(10)

iv. Where a Will is made by a blind or illiterate testator and there is no evidence that the testator knows or understands the content of the Will.

Thus:

"Before admitting Will to proof, a Will which appears to have been signed by a blind or illiterate

testator or by another person by direction of the testator, or which for any other reason give rise to doubt as to the testator having had knowledge of the contents of the Will at the time of its execution, the Registrar shall satisfy himself that the testator has such knowledge"(11)

v. Where a Will is not dated or the date is incomplete.

Thus:
"Where there is doubt as to the date on which a Will was executed, the Registrar may require such evidence as he thinks necessary to establish the date."(12)

PERFECTION OF IRREGULARITIES IN WILLS

From the foregoing Rules, various affidavit evidence are required to perfect irregularities observed in Examination of Wills. It is of importance to note that every affidavit used in Probate matters must satisfy the requirements of the Evidence Act on Affidavits.(13)Also, the Registrar may require viva voce evidence of persons making affidavit if he deems fit.

Therefore:

"In every case where evidence is directed or allowed to be given by affidavit, the Court may require the personal attendance of the deponent, if within the jurisdiction, before the Court to be examined viva voce respecting the manner of his affidavit. The examination may take place before any affidavit has been sworn or prepared if the Court thinks fit."(14)

Basically, the Registrar will not issue Probate or Administration with the Will annexed, until all inquiries which he deems fit to institute have been answered to his satisfaction. Therefore, where Wills imperfectly executed are perfected, Probate or Administration with the Will annexed may be granted.

REFERENCES

(1) That is, regularized, cleared off or resolved.

(2) Or.59 R.15, R.16 & R.17 (Edo) 2018: R.15-Execution of Will of blind or illiterate Testator. R.16-Evidence as to terms, conditions and date of execution of Will. R.17-Attempted revocation of Will.

(3) Or.59 R.18 (Edo) 2018; Or.55 R.18 (Delta) 2009 and Or.58 R.9 (Lagos) 2012, supra.

(4) Or.59 R.33 (Edo) 2018; Or.55 R.33 (Delta) and Or.58 R.5(3) (Lagos) 2012, supra.

(5) Or.59 R.14(3) (Edo) 2018; Or.55 R.14(3) (Delta) 2009 and Or.58 R.5(3) 2012, supra.

(6) Or.59 R.31(1) (Edo) 2018; Or.55 R.31(1) (Delta) 2009 and Or.58 R.4(1) (Lagos) 2012, supra.

(7) Garner, B, A., "Black's Law Dictionary", supra pg. 147.

(8) Or.59 R.14(1)(2), R.32 and Or.58 R.20(1) (Edo) 2018; Or.55 R.14(1)(2), R.32 and Or.54 R.20(1) (Delta) 2009 and Or.58 R.5(1)(2) & R.6 (Lagos), supra.

(9) Or.58 R.20(2) ibid and Or.54 R.20(2) ibid.

(10) Or.58 R.25(3) & OR.59 R.37(2) (Edo) 2018; Or.54 R.25(3) & Or.55 R.37(2) (Delta) and Or.58 R.12(2) (Lagos).

(11) Or.59 R.15, R.35 and Or.58 R.23 (Edo) 2018; Or.55 R.15, R.35 and Or.54 R. 23 (Delta) 2009 and Or.58 R,10 (Lagos), supra.

(12) Or.59 R.16(3) (Edo) 2018; Or.55 R.16(3) (Delta) 2009 and Or.58 R,7(2) (Lagos), supra.

(13) Or.59 R.76 (Edo) 2018 and Or.55 R.76 (Delta) 2009.

(14) Or.59 R.4O (Edo) 2018 and Or.55 R.40 (Delta) 2009. NOTE: VIVA VOCE EVIDENCE refer to oral testimony or evidence. NOTE: Oral Evidence throws more light on

Documentary Evidence- see the case of Ndule V. Ojiakor (2013) 30 WRN Pp 41. However Oral Evidence becomes more credible when supported by Documentary Evidence. -see the case of Odutola V. Mabogunje (2013) 53 NSCQR pg.57.

CHAPTER FIFTEEN

PROBATE

Wills must go through Probate in order to transfer ownership of assets owned by the Testator to his living Beneficiaries. Therefore the only way to legally transfer assets in accordance with a Will is through the Probate process. The grant obtained by Executors named in a Testator's Will is known as Probate. Probate is the authority that validates the power and functions of an Executor, although the authority of an Executor to act is first derived from the Will.

After the reading of a Testator's Will, forms for Probate can be obtained upon application to the Registrar, from either the Executors [(1)] or the legal representative of the Testator's estate.

Thus:

> *"When any person subject to the jurisdiction of the Court dies, all petitions for the grant of Probate of his Will and all applications on other matter connected with it, shall be made to the Probate Registrar of the Court at Benin City."* [(2)]

PROCEDURE FOR GRANT OF PROBATE

Upon the receipt of application for Probate forms and the subsequent examination of the Will by the Registrar and if he is satisfied that the Will was properly executed and can be admitted to proof, the following forms are issued to the applicants:

i. Application for Probate or Letters of Administration
ii. Inventory form
iii. Bank certificate
iv. Oath for Executor
v. Affidavit of Attesting Witness

The above forms are issued by a forwarding letter stating the oath and filing fee regarding each of the forms.(3) Once these forms have been completed and returned, they are checked to ensure that the names of the Testator, Executors and Witnesses on the Will and that on the completed forms are the same. Where there is any discrepancy, affidavit of identity must be called for. If the forms are correctly filled, Oath and filing fees are paid, the Executors and the Witnesses (usually two) are made to appear and sign on their respective forms before the Commissioner for Oath.

Thereafter, the letter demanding for assessment and valuation reports on the Testator's real properties are prepared.(4) Immediately the Registrar receive reply to such letter and also knowing the amount outstanding to the credit or debit of the Testator's bank account and the value of his shares, if any, the Registrar can then ascertain the gross value of the Testator's estate and also assess the estate fee. As soon as the estate fee is assessed, the Executors or the legal representative of the Testator's estate are notified and requested to tender a bank draft in favour of the Registrar, with the amount stated in the notification or remittance letter, as estate fee.

On payment of estate fee chargeable on the Testator's estate, Minute and Order are prepared, praying the Chief Judge for approval of grant of Probate. Once the Chief Judge grants the prayer to issue Probate of both the real and personal property of the Testator to the Executors named in the Will, the grant, "Probate" is prepared and signed by the Registrar.

The grant must contain the following:

i. The Testator's estate file number;
ii. The effective date of the grant;
iii. The name of the Testator;

iv. The date and place of death;
v. The Testator's native place and fixed place of abode;[5]
vi. The names and addresses of the Executors;
vii. The estate sworn to;
viii. The red seal and the seal of the Registry;
ix. The Registrar's signature.

At the back of the grant, the fees payable, the purposes for such payments and receipt numbers issued are recorded. Attached to the grant, is a Certified True Copy of the Testator's Will. The grant is made in three copies and the original copy of the grant is given to the Executors.

It is important to note that in the estate of a deceased who died leaving a Will, persons entitled to a grant of Probate or Administration With Will Annexed are usually determined in accordance with Order of Priority.[6]

CODICILS

A codicil may be defined as a writing by the Testator intended as a supplement or addition to his Will, not necessarily disposing of the entire estate but modifying, explaining or otherwise qualifying the Will in some way.[7]

EFFECT OF CODICILS IN RELATION TO WILLS

The effect of a codicil in relation to a Testator's Will may be either of the following:

i. To enlarge or restrict the provisions of the Will; [8]
ii. To annul or revoke a Will altogether;
iii. It may explain or alter, confirm or revoke the Will wholly or in part;

iv. Where the Will itself is invalid, may by a valid re-execution and republication revive and renew the Will.

It is very important to know that, the provisions of the Law and Procedures relating to Wills apply equally to Codicils.[9] Thus when admitted to Probate, the Codicil becomes a part of the Will.

GRANT IN RESPECT OF CODICIL AND COPY OF WILL WHERE THE ORIGINAL WILL IS NOT AVAILABLE

An application for an order, admitting to proof a Codicil or a Will contained in a copy, a completed draft, a reconstruction or other evidence of its contents where the original Will is not available, may be made to the Registrar. However, where a Will is not available owing to its being retained in the custody of a Foreign Court or another State Probate Registry, a duly authenticated copy of the Will may be admitted to proof without any such Order.[10]

The application for such grant must be supported by an affidavit setting out the grounds of the application and any other evidence as the applicant can adduce as to:

i. The due execution of the Will;
ii. Its existence after the death of the Testator;
iii. The accuracy of the copy or other evidence of the contents of the Will; together with any consent in writing to the application given by any person not under disability who would be prejudiced by the grant.

PROCEDURE FOR GRANT WHERE ORIGINAL WILL IS NOT AVAILABLE

A Will deposited and read in one State or Country can be admitted to proof in another State or Country. For example, a Will deposited and read in the Probate Registry of Lagos State, can be admitted to proof in Probate Registry of Edo State

Therefore, any person who intend to prove a copy of a Testator's Codicil or Will of which the original is not available, owing to its being retained in the custody of a foreigner court or in another state Probate Registry, can apply to the Registrar to that effect. Attached to such application include:

i. A certified true copy of medical certificate of the Testator's death or proof of death;
ii. Two (2) certified true copies of the said Codicil or Will
iii. A certified true copy of the application for the reading of Will made to the Registrar of the Registry where the Will was read.
iv. A certified true copy of invitation letter for the reading of the Will.
v. A certified true copy of the attendance list of those present when the Will was read.

As soon as the application is approved, the process of proving the Will commences and if the Registrar is satisfied that the Will is properly executed and can be admitted to proof, Probate forms are issued and proceeded with. It is important to note that such Codicil or Will must contain provisions relating to personal or real property within the jurisdiction of the proving state.[(11)]

CUSTODY OF WILLS OF WHICH PROBATE IS GRANTED

The word custody may be defined as the care and control of a thing or person for inspection, preservation or security.

Under the Probate Rules, every Original Will of which Probate or Letters of Administration With Will Annexed is granted must be filed and kept in the Probate Registry in such manner as to secure the due preservation and convenient inspection of same.[12]

A copy of every such Will and of the Probate or Letters of Administration must be preserved in a book kept for the purpose in the Registry. No Original Will can be delivered out for any purpose without the direction in writing of the Court where the Will is lodged. However, a certified true copy under the seal of the Court of the Probate or Administration with the Will annexed can be obtained from the Registry. [13]

DOUBLE PROBATE

Double Probate is where two grant of Probate in relation to the same Will and Estate can co-exist and run concurrently, that is; the Original Grant and the Double Probate. This grant is available for an Executor who, although willing to act, has been hindered by certain circumstances from teaming up with his co-Executors to obtain Probate originally. [14]

Double Probate may arise where preservation of "Right" exists, for example:

i. Where an Executor who was a minor (less than eighteen (18) years) when his co-Executor(s) obtained Probate desires to take office and applies to be issued a grant on attaining "majority"; that is eighteen (18) years and above.

ii. When an Executor of full age and willing to act was abroad or residence outside the jurisdiction of the court when his co-Executor(s) took out Probate, finally returns to the state and still willing to act, applies for a grant.

It is important to know that where the estate fee had been fully paid on the property of the deceased before the issue of the first grant (Probate), no further duty may be charged again. The value of the estate is to be sworn as the value of the assets remaining unadministered at the date of requesting for the second grant (Double Probate). However fees for filing of documents, certification, marking of will and for making oath on relevant papers may be charged by the Registrar.

LIABILITY OF EXECUTOR NEGLECTING TO APPLY FOR PROBATE

It is the duty of every Executor of a Will read to apply for Probate and prove such Will. Thus, the Court may of its own motion or upon the application of any person claiming an interest under a Will, give notice to the Executors, to apply to prove the Will or to renounce Probate. The Executors or any one of them must within (21) twenty one days after the notice, apply for Probate or renounced accordingly.(15)

Therefore, if any person named Executor in the Will of a Testator, takes possession and administers or otherwise deals with any part of the Testator's estate and does not apply for Probate within one month after the death of the Testator or after the termination of any suit or dispute relating to Probate or Administration, the Executor may, independently of any other liability, be deemed guilty of contempt of Court and will be liable to a fine, not exceeding ₦50,000.00 (fifty thousand naira).(16)

UNAUTHORIZED PERSON INTERMEDDLING WITH DECEASED'S ESTATE

Where a person subject to the jurisdiction of the Court dies intestate, his estate is deemed to have been vested, on the Chief Judge, from the date of his death until Administration is granted.(17)

The Chief Judge is equally empowered to request the Court of any Judicial Division to take measures and make such orders as may appear necessary or expedient for the interim preservation of the property of the deceased within such Judicial Division for the discovery or preservation of the Will of the deceased or for any other purpose connected with the duties of the Court under Probate Rules and every Court must carry out any such request as far as practicable and report to the Chief Judge.(18)

Thus:

> *"The Court shall, when the circumstance of the case appear to require forth with on the death of a person or as soon after, appoint and authorize an officer of the Court, or some other fit person, to take possession of his property within its jurisdiction, or put it under seal, and so keep it until it can be dealt with according to law."*(19)

Therefore, if any person other than:

i. The person named Ẹxecutor or Administrator; or
ii. An officer of the Court or person authorized by the Court.

Takes possession of and administers or otherwise deals with the property of any deceased person, he will, besides the other liabilities he may incur, be liable to such fine not exceeding ₦50,000.00 (fifty thousand naira) as the Court having regard to the condition of the person so interfering with the property and the other circumstances of the case, may deem fit to impose.[(20)]

EXECUTOR DE SON TORT

The term "Executor De Son Tort" is a French word for "Executor of his own wrong".[(21)] In general terms, it is used to describe a person who without legal authority takes on the responsibility to act as an Executor or Administrator of a deceased's estate, usually to the detriment of the estate's beneficiaries or creditors.

Thus, he that takes upon himself the office of an Executor by intrusion, not being so appointed by the Testator, is called "EXECUTOR DE SON TORT" and has committed a breach.

Therefore:

> *"If any person to the defrauding of creditors or without full valuable consideration, obtains, receives or hold any real or personal estate of a deceased person or effects the released of any debt or liability due to the estate of the deceased, he shall be charged as executor in his own wrong to the extent of the real and personal estate received or coming to his hands, or the debt or liability released, after deducting -*
>
> (a) Any debt for valuable consideration and without fraud due to him from the deceased person at the time of his death and
>
> (b) Any payment made by him which might properly be made by a personal representative."[(22)]

REFERENCES

(1) Persons named by a Testator to carry out the instructions in the Testator's Will. They are not more than four (4). See section24 AEL (Bendel) 1976, supra.

(2) Or.59R.6(1) (Edo) 2018; Or.55 R.6(1) (Delta) 2009 and Or.57 R.1(1)(Lagos) 2012, supra.

(3) See Appendix 28 for specimen of Letter forwarding forms for Probate.

(4) It is the duty of the Permanent Secretary, Ministry of Lands to assign a valuation officer who will inspect and ascertain the value of each of the Testator's real properties listed.

(5) The Testator fixed place of abode must be within the jurisdiction of the Court, that is, within Edo State.

(6) Or.59 R.21 (Edo) 2018 and Or.55 R.21 (Delta) 2009, supra.

(7) Codicil is from the word " Codicillus", a Latin word for " Little document, book or writing"- see Garner, B. A., " Black's Law Dictionary ", supra pg.294.

(8) It may add to or subtract from the provisions of the Will.

(9) Or.58 R.27(2)& Or.59 R.39(2) (Edo) 2018 and Or.54 R.27(2)& Or.55 R.39(2) (Delta) 2009, supra.

(10) Or.59 R.66 (Edo) 2018 and Or.55 R.66 (Delta) 2009, supra.

(11) That is, evidence why the Will is desired to be proved in Edo State.

(12) Or.58R.17& Or.59 R.29 (Edo) 2018; Or.54 R.17 & Or.55 R.29 (Delta) 2009 and Or.58 R.2 (Lagos) 2012, supra.

(13) Or.58 R.18 & Or.59 R.30 (Edo) 2018; Or.54 R.18 &Or.55 R.30 (Delta) 2009 and Or.58 R.3 (Lagos) 2012, supra.

(14) Mosanya, J. A., "Common Form Probate Business", supra pgs. 60-64.

(15) Or.58 R.7 & Or.59 R.4(Edo) 2018; Or54 R.7& Or.55 R.4 (Delta) 2009 and Or.58 R.18 (Lagos) 2012, supra.

(16) Or.58 R.8 & Or.59 R.5 (Edo) 2018; Or.54 R.8& Or.55 R.5 (Delta) 2009 and Or.58 R.19 (Lagos) 2012. NOTE: Under the Lagos State Rules, such application for Probate must be made within three (3) months.

(17) See section 10 AEL (Bendel) 1976, supra.

(18) Or.58 R.1(2) & Or.59 R.6(2) (Edo) 2018 and Or.54 R.1(2)& Or.55 R.6(2) 2009, supra. NOTE: Probate Rules means rules and orders for regulating the procedure and practice of High Court in regard to non-contentious or common form probate business- see section 2 AEL (Bendel) 1976, supra.

(19) Or.58 R.2 (Edo) 2018; Or.54 R.2 (Delta) 2009and Or.57 R.2(1) (Lagos) 2012, supra.

(20) Or.58 R.3 (Edo) 2018; Or.54 R.3 (Delta) 2009 and Or.57 R.17 (Lagos) 2012, supra.

(21) Garner, B. A., "Black's Law Dictionary ", supra, pg.651.

(22) Section 18 AEL (Bendel) 1976, supra. For Liability of estate of personal representative-see section 19 AEL (Bendel) 1976, supra.

CHAPTER SIXTEEN

ADMINISTRATION WITH WILL ANNEXED

The Grant obtained by persons interested in the Testator's estate, other than the Executors, is known as Letters of Administration (With Will Annexed).

Letters of Administration With Will Annexed, is a process of appointing Administrators in respect of a Testator's estate, either because his Will does not name an Executor or the named Executor does not qualify. This type of Administration may be obtained by a Court Order, appointing persons named in the Order to be Administrators and requesting the Registrar to issue Letters of Administration (With Will Annexed) to such persons.

Therefore:

> *"Where a person has died intestate as to his personal estate or leaving a Will affecting personal estate, but without having appointed an executor thereof willing and competent to take probate, or where the executor shall at the time of the death of such person be resident out of the jurisdiction and it shall appear to the Court to be necessary or convenient in any such case to appoint some person to be administrator of the personal estate of the deceased or of any part thereof, the Court may appoint such person as it shall think fit, to be such administrator upon his giving such security, if any, as the Court shall direct and every such administrator may be limited as the Court shall think fit."*[(1)]

It can also be obtain upon an application to the Registrar, either by the beneficially interested persons or the legal representative of the Testator's estate, if the Registrar is satisfy due to reason of exceptional circumstances, in the absence of a proving or surviving executor. Also it can be obtained upon a resolution or instrumental document collectively signed by all beneficially interested persons in the Testator's estate.

Therefore:

i. "Where all the people entitled to the estate of a deceased under a Will have assigned their whole interest in the estate to one or more persons, the assignee or assignees shall replace in the order of priority for a grant of probate, the assignor or if there are two or more assignors, the assignors with the highest priority, in the absence of a proving executor.

ii. Where there are two or more assignees, probate may be granted with the consent of the others to anyone or more (not exceeding four) of them.

iii. In any case where probate is applied for by an assignee, a copy of the instrument of assignment shall be lodged in the registry."(2)

Where the beneficial interest in the whole estate of a deceased is vested absolutely in a person who has renounced his right to a grant of Letters of Administration with the Will annexed, and has consented to such Administration being granted to the person or persons who would be entitled to his estate if he himself had died intestate, Administration may be granted to such person or more (not exceeding four).(3)

INSTANCES FOR ISSUING LETTERS OF ADMINISTRATION (WITH WILL ANNEXED)

Letters of Administration (With Will Annexed) may be issued in the following circumstances:

i. Where the Testator does not appoint executor in his Will

ii. Where the Executors named in the Will are residents of another country at the time of Testator's death and it appears to be necessary or convenient to appoint some persons to administer the Testator's estate.[(4)]

iii. Where the Executors appointed in the Will predeceased the Testator.[(5)]

iv. Where Executors appointed in the Will of a Testator died before proving the Will.

Thus:

> *"Where a person appointed executor in a Will survives the testator, but either dies without having taken Probate, or having been called on by the Court to take probate, does not appear, his right in respect of the executorships wholly ceases and without further renunciation, the representation to the Testator and the administration of his property may go on and be committed as if that person had not been appointed executor."*[(6)]

v. Where the appointment of executor is void for uncertainty or irregularity.

Therefore:

> *"Unless the Registrar otherwise directs, probate or administration with the Will attached, shall be granted to a living person in preference to the personal representative of a deceased person who would, if living, be entitled in the same degree, and*

to a person not under disability in preference to an infant entitled in the same degree." [(7)]

vi. Where the executor appointed is an infant at the time of the Testator's death.

Thus:

> *"Where an infant who is a sole executor has no interest in the residuary estate of the deceased, administration with the Will attached for the use and benefit of the infant until he attains the age of eighteen years shall, unless the Registrar otherwise directs be granted to the person entitled to the residuary estate."*[(8)]

vii. Where the executor appointed is incompetent by reason of mental or physical incapacity.

Thus:

"(1) Where the Registrar is satisfied that a person entitled to a grant is by reason of mental or physical incapacity, incapable of managing his affairs, a grant for his use and benefit limited during his incapacity or in such other way as the Registrar may direct, may be made:

(a) In the case of mental incapacity, to the person authorized by the court to apply for probate; or

(b) Where there is no person so authorized or in the case of physical incapacity –

(i) If the person incapable is entitled as executor and has

no interest in the residuary estate of the deceased, to the person entitled to such residuary estate.

(ii) If the person incapable is entitled otherwise than as executor or is an executor having an interest in the residuary estate of the deceased, to the person who would be entitled to a grant in respect of his estate if he had died intestate; or to such other person as the Registrar may by order direct."[9]

It is of interest to note that unless the Registrar otherwise directs:

(a) No grant shall be made under the foregoing rule unless all persons entitled in the same degree as the person incapable, have been considered and excluded.[10]

(b) In the case of mental incapacity, notice of intended application for a grant under this rule must be given to the person alleged to be so incapable.[11]

(viii) Where the executor renounce probate: No person who has renounced a grant in one capacity may obtain a grant in some other capacity, unless the Registrar otherwise directs.[12]Although, a Renunciation of Probate or Administration may be retracted at any time on the Order of the Registrar, however, only in exceptional circumstances, may leave be given to an Executor to retract a Renunciation of Probate after a grant has been made to some other person entitled in a lower degree.[13] It is of great importance to know that:

(i) Renunciation of Probate by an Executor does not operate as renunciation of any right which he may have to grant of Letters of Administration in some other capacity unless he expressly renounces such right. [14]

(ii) An infant's right to administration may be renounced only by person assigned as guardian. [15] However, an infant executor's right to Probate on attaining the age of eighteen (18) years may not be renounced by any person on his behalf.[16]

(iii) Where an executor who has renounced probate has been permitted to withdraw the renunciation and prove the Will, the Probate shall take effect and be deemed always to have taken effect without prejudice to the previous acts and dealings of and notices to any other personal representatives who has previously proved the Will or taken out letters of administration and a memorandum of subsequent probate shall be endorse on the original probate or letters of administration.[17]

(iv) In the estate of a deceased who died leaving a Will, persons entitled to a grant of Probate or Letters of Administration with the Will Annexed are determined in accordance with Order of Priority.[18] Equally related to the Order of Priority for grant, is the exception to the rule as to priority.[19]

PROCEDURE FOR GRANTOF LETTERS OFADMINISTRATION (WITH WILL ANNEXED)

In obtaining Letters of Administration (With Will Annexed), the same procedure leading to the grant of letters of Administration (Without Will) is followed.

However, Letters of Administration (With Will Annexed) attract single publication of application and also the second set of forms, though similar to that of letters of administration (Without Will), but the headings are different for example, Administration Bond (With Will Annexed), Oath for Administration. (With Will Annexed)

Once the grant is prepared, signed and ready for collection, a certified true copy of the Testator's Will is attached. No grant of Letters of Administration With Will Annexed can be issued within seven (7) days of the death of the deceased.(20)

It is crucially important to know that persons to whom Letters of Administration (With Will Annexed) is granted, are under statutory obligation to carry out the provisions of the Will in like manner as if grant of Probate had been granted to Executors.(21)

Thus:

> *"Every person to whom administration of the real and personal estate of a deceased person is granted shall, subject to the limitations contained in the grant, have the same rights and liabilities and be accountable in like manner as if he were the executor of the deceased."*(22)

RFERENCES

(1) Or.58 R.37 (Edo) 2018; Or.54 R.37 (Delta) 2009 and Or.59 R.9 (Lagos) 2012, supra.

(2) Or.59 R.41 (Edo) 2018; Or.55 R.41 (Delta) 2009 and Or.58 R.22 (Lagos), supra.

(3) Or.59 R.46 (Edo) 2018; Or.55 R.46 (Delta) 2009 and Or.58 R.24 (Lagos) 2012, supra.

(4) Or.58 R.37 (Edo) 2018; Or.54 R.37 (Delta) 2009 and Or.59 R.9 (Lagos) 2012, supra.

(5) It is advisable that the Executors and Witnesses must not be older than the Testator.

(6) Or.58 R.26 & Or. 59 R.38 (Edo) 2018; Or.54 R.26 & Or.55 R.38 (Delta) 2009 and Or.58 R.13 (Lagos) 2012, supra.

(7) Or.59 R.44(4) (Edo) 2018; Or.55 R.44(4) (Delta) 2009 and Or.59 R.13(4) (Lagos) 2012, supra.

(8) Or.59 R.49(5) (Edo) 2018; Or.55R.49(5) (Delta) 2009 and Or.57R.12(5) (Lagos) 2012,supra.

(9) Or.59R.51(1) (Edo) 2018; Or.55 R.51(1) (Delta) 2009 and Or.57R.14(1) (Lagos) 2012, supra.

(10) Or.59 R.51(2) ibid; Or.55 R.51(2) ibid and Or.57 R.14(2) ibid.

(11) Or.59 R.51(3) ibid; Or.55R.51(3) ibid and Or.57 R.14(3) ibid. NOTE: Under the Lagos Rules, Notice of intended application is given to the Guardian of the person alleged to be so incapable.

(12) Or.59 R.52(2) (Edo) 2018; Or.55 R.52(2) (Delta) 2009 and Or.58 R.25(2) (Lagos) 2012, supra.

(13) Or.59 R.52(3) ibid; Or.55 R.52(3) ibid and Or.58 R.25(3) ibid.

(14) Or.59 R.52(1) ibid; Or.55 R.52(1) and Or.58 R.25(1) ibid.

(15) Or.59 R.49(6) (Edo) 2018; Or.55 R.49(6) (Delta) 2009 and Or.57 R.12(6) ibid.

(16) Or.59 R.50(2) (Edo) 2018; Or.55 R.50(2) (Delta) 2009 and Or.57 R.13(2) (Lagos) 2012, supra.

(17) Section 7(1) AEL (Bendel) 1976.

(18) Or.59 R.21 (Edo) 2018; Or.55 R.21 (Delta) 2009 and Or.58 R.23 (Lagos) 2012, supra.

(19) Or.59 R.45 (Edo) 2018 and Or.55 R.45 (Delta) 2009.

(20) Or.58 R.1(3) (Edo) 2018; Or.54 R.1(3) (Delta) 2009 and Or.57 R.1(2) (Lagos) 2012. NOTE: Under the Lagos Rules, within fourteen (14) days.

(21) See Section 30 AEL (Bendel) 1976.

(22) Section 13, ibid.

CHAPTER SEVENTEEN

LIMITED ADMINISTRATION

The word limited may be defined as the extent of power, right or authority. Administration is the management and settlement of the estate of an Intestate deceased or of a Testator, who has no Executor, by a person legally appointed and supervised by the Court. The Administration of the estate of a deceased involves:

i. Realizing the deceased's assets;
ii. The payment of debts and other claims against the estate; and
iii. The division and distribution of what remains.

Thus, an Administration granted for temporary period or for a special purpose, is known as Limited Administration.(1) Limited Administration can also be referred to as Limited Probate. Limited Probate is made to an Executor or Administrator whose powers, right or authority is limited either as regards the property of the deceased or as to time. For example, where Executor or Administrator is appointed for a period after the death of the deceased or for a particular purpose.

Therefore, Limited Administration can be for temporary period (Temporary Administration) or for special purpose (Special Administration).(2)

i. Temporary Administration – An Administration in which the Court appoints a fiduciary to administer the affairs of a deceased's estate for a short time before an Administrator or Executor can be appointed or qualified.(3)

ii. Special Administration – An administration with authority to deal with only some of the deceased's property as opposed to administering the entire estate.

TYPES OF LIMITED ADMINISTRATION

Under the Edo State High Court [Civil Procedure] Rules, 2018 there are various types of Limited Administration, some of which include the following:

i. Grant To Attorneys;
ii. Grant On Behalf Of Infants;
iii. Grant In Case Of Mental Or Physical Incapacity;
iv. Grant To Administer Part Of An Estate;
v. Grant Of Administration Colligenda Bona;
vi. Grant Durante Absentia;
vii. Grant To Officers;
viii. Grant To Consular Or Person Authorized By Him To Administer Estate.

GRANT TO ATTORNEYS

A lawfully appointed attorney of a person entitled to a grant can apply and obtain grant on behalf of such person.

Therefore:

"(1) Where a person entitled to a grant resides outside the state, a grant may be made to his lawfully constituted attorney, for his use and benefit, limited until such person shall obtain a grant or in such other way as the Registrar may direct:

Provide that where the person so entitled is an executor, administration shall not be granted to his attorney without notice to the other executors, if any.

(2) Where the Registrar is satisfied by affidavit that it is desirable for a grant to be made to the lawfully constituted attorney of a person entitled to a grant and resident in the State, he may direct that a grant be made to the attorney for the use and benefit of such person, limited until such person shall obtain a grant or in such other way as the Registrar may direct."[4]

GRANT ON BEHALF OF INFANTS

Where the person to whom a grant would otherwise be made is an infant, a grant for his use and benefit until he attains the age of eighteen years may be granted to both parents of the infant or any guardian appointed by a Court of competent jurisdiction and if there is no such guardian able and willing to act and the infant has attained the age of sixteen years, to any next-of-kin nominated by the infant.[5]

GRANT IN CASE OF MENTAL OR PHYSICAL INCAPACITY

Where the Registrar is satisfied that a person entitled to a grant is by reason of mental or physical incapacity, incapable of managing his affairs, a grant for his use and benefit, limited during his incapacity or in such other way, may be made to any of the following persons:

i. The person authorized by the Court to apply for the grant;
ii. The person entitled to such residuary estate;[6]
iii. The person who would be entitled to a grant in respect of his estate, if he had died intestate;

iv. Such other person as the Registrar may by order direct;(7)

GRANT TO ADMINISTER PART OF AN ESTATE

An application for an order for a grant limited to part of an estate may be made to the Registrar and must be supported by an affidavit stating:

(a) Whether the application is made in respect of the real estate only or any part thereof, or real estate together with personal estate, or in respect of a trust estate only;
(b) Whether the estate of the deceased is known to be insolvent;
(c) That the persons entitled to a grant in respect of the whole estate in priority to the applicant have been considered and excluded.(8)

Therefore, by the provision of the above rule, an application to suspend the Administration of part of deceased's estate already declared on the inventory form filed in the Registry, can be made.

SUSPENDING THE ADMINISTRATION OF PART OF DECEASED'S ESTATE

Sometimes, applicants encounter difficulties in getting reply to letters calling for figures, especially, the difficulties involved in tracing deceased's record of service file in pension office or the movement of such file from the deceased's place of work to pension office, finding deceased's shares certificates, dividend slips or obtaining current central security clearing system (CSCS) account print out and Pension Managers' retirement savings account (RSA) print out etc., thereby creating unnecessary delay in the process of obtaining grant.

However, by Probate Rules,[9]applicants in any of the above mentioned dilemma, can apply to suspend that particular estate and proceed with other estate intended to be administered.

PROCEDURE FOR SUSPENDING THE ADMINISTRATION OF PART OF DECEASED'S ESTATE

Applicant who intends to suspend the Administration of part of the deceased estate already declared in the inventory form filed must apply to the Registrar for such request. The application must be supported by an affidavit, stating the part of the deceased's estate intended to be suspended and the reasons for the suspension. In personal representation, the affidavit is sworn to by one of the applicants,[10] where the applicants are legally represented, either the legal practitioner or any of the applicants. Once the application is approved by the Registrar, applicants are allowed to proceed with the other estate declared on the inventory form filed.

However, if the difficulty associated with the suspended estate is resolved before the signing of the grant, it may form part of the estate to be administered. But where the difficulty is resolve after the signing of the grant, such suspended estate, can only be administered via Additional Asset.[11]

GRANT OF ADMINISTRATION AD COLLIGENDA BONA

The term "Ad Colligenda Bona" is a Latin word for collecting goods. The grant of Administration Ad Colligenda Bona is a special Letters of Administration authorizing a person to collect and preserve a deceased's property.[12] In other words, it is an authorization from a Judicial Officer to an approved person to collect and maintain the property of a person who died intestate.

Thus:

> *"An application for an Order, for a grant of administration ad Colligenda bona, may be made to the Registrar, and shall be supported by an affidavit setting out the grants of the application"*(13)

Therefore, Administrator Ad Colligendum Bona is an Administrator appointed solely to collect and preserve the deceased's estate.

GRANT DURANTE ABSENTIA

Grant Durante Absentia is an Administration granted during the absence of either the Executor or the person who has precedence as Administrator.

Thus:

> *"An application for an order, for a grant of special administration where a personal representative is residing outside the state, shall be made to the Court, on motions."*(14)

Similarly;

> *"If at the expiration of twelve months from the death of a person any personal representative of the deceased to whom a grant has been made is residing out of Nigeria, the court may, on the application of any creditor or person interested in the estate of the deceased, grant to him in the prescribed form special administration of the estate of the deceased."* (15)

Therefore, Administrator Durante Absentia is an Administrator appointed to act while an Executor or Administrator with precedence is temporarily absent.

GRANT TO OFFICERS

In intestacy,[16]where the special circumstances of the case appear to the Court so to require, the Court may, if it deems fit, on the application of any person having interest in the estate of the deceased or of its own motion, grant Letters of Administration to:

i. An Officer of the Court;
ii. A Consular Officer;
iii. A Person in the service of the Government.

The Officer or person so appointed must act under the supervision of the Court and will be indemnified.[17] He must file in the Court, the accounts of his Administration at intervals not exceeding three month.[18]

GRANT TO CONSULAR OR PERSON AUTHORIZED BY HIM

Grants to consular or person authorized by him is related to the Administration of estate of foreign citizen.

Any citizen of a country other than Nigeria, who died without leaving within the jurisdiction a spouse or next-of-kin and had his usual place of residence within a Government station, the Magistrate having jurisdiction within such station or the Local Government Secretary in charge of the station in which he died, will collect and secure all monies and other property belonging to the deceased and then request the Secretary to the Government to inform the nearest consular officer of the deceased's country, of the death of the deceased and transmit to him the money and property.

Where it is declared that the Local Government Secretary will collect and secure all money and other property of the deceased, such Local Government Secretary may appoint an Administrative Officer attached to his Local Government or of another Local Government or a Magistrate to act in his place.(19)

Thus, application may be made to the Court by any such Consular Officer or by any person authorized by him, in writing and under the consular seal, for leave of Court to administer the estate of the deceased. The Court may make such Order as to security for payment of debts and the method of Administration as the Court deems fit and vary such Order when and so often as is expedient.(20)

From the various aforementioned Probate Rules, the following can be deduced in relation to Limited Administration:

(i) Right to grant is reserved. For example:-

(a) Grants to attorneys

"..........for his use and benefit, limited until such person shall obtain a grant or in such other way as the Registrar may direct."(21)

(b) Grants on behalf of infants:-

"............ grants for his use and benefit until he attains the age of eighteen years ....."(22)

(c) Grants in case of mental or physical incapacity

"........ a grant for his use and benefit, limited during his incapacity....."(23)

(ii) Administration of the estate of the deceased is temporary, for example:

(a) Grants to Attorneys;

(b) Grants on behalf of infants;

(c) Grants in cases of mental or physical incapacity etc.

(iii) Administration can be limited to part of a deceased's estate as opposed to the entire estate. For example: Grants to administer part of an estate.

It is of great importance to know that where a grant of Administration is Limited to either the real or personal property of the deceased, the Administrator has no power to administer the property (real or personal) not covered by the grant.(24)

(iv) Administration can be for a specific or special purpose, for example: Grants Durante Absentia and Grants of Administration Ad Colligenda Bona etc.

In granting administration, the Court usually have regard to the rights of all persons interested in the estate of the deceased or the proceeds of sale thereof and in particular, Administration with the Will annexed may be granted to a devisee or legatee,(25) and any such Administration may be limited in any way the Court deems fit. (26)

However, if by reason of the insolvency of the estate of the deceased or any other special circumstances, it appears to the Court to be necessary or expedient to appoint as Administrator some person other than the person who by Law is entitled to the grant of Administration, the Court may in its discretion, appoint as Administrator such person as it deems expedient and any such Administration granted, may be limited in any way the Court deems fits.(27)

Also generally regarded as Limited Administration are:

(a) Grants of Administration De Bonis Non;
(b) Grants of Administration De Bonis Non Cum Testamento Annexo;
(c) Caeterorum Administration;
(d) Grants of Administration Pendente Lite.

ADMINISTRATION DE BONIS NON

The term "De Bonis Non" is a Latin word for "of the goods not administered." Grants of Administration De Bonis Non is an Administration granted for the purpose of settling the remainder of an Intestate estate that was not administered by the former Administrator.[(28)]

In other words, when the first Administrator of an intestate estate dies or is removed, the subsequent Administrator is called an Administrator Bonis Non, who administers the goods not administer by the previous Administrator.

ADMINISTRATION DE BONIS NON CUM TESTAMENTO ANNEXO

This is an Administration granted to settle the reminder of a Testate estate not settled by a previous Administrator or Executor.[(29)]This type of Administration arises when there is a valid Will, as opposed to an Administration De Bonis Non, which is granted when there is no Will.

CAETERORUM ADMINISTRATION

"Caeterorum" is a Latin word for "of the rest". Caeterorum Administration is an Administration granted when Limited powers previously granted to an Administrator are inadequate to settle the estate's residue. [(30)]

ADMINISTRATION PENDENTE LITE

This type of Administration is granted during the pendency of a Suit concerning a Will's validity. It is also termed Pendente Lite Administration or Special Administration.

Thus:

> *"Where any legal proceedings touching the validity of the Will of a deceased person, or for obtaining, recalling or revoking any grant, are pending, the court may grant administration of the estate of the deceased to an administrator, who shall have all the rights and powers of a general administrator other than the right of distributing the residue of the estate, and every such administrator shall be subject to the immediate control of the court and act under its direction."* (31)

REFERENCES

(1) Garner, B. A., "Black's Law Dictionary", supra pg. 50.

(2) Ibid.

(3) A "Fiduciary" is one who must exercise a high standard of care in managing another's money or property- ibid, pg.702

(4) Or.59 R.48 (Edo) 2018; Or.55 R.48 (Delta) 2009 and Or.57 R.11 (Lagos) 2012, supra.

(5) Or.59 R.49 (Edo) 2018; Or.55 R.49 (Delta) 2009 and Or.57 R.12 (Lagos) 2012, supra.

(6) If the person incapable is entitled as Executor and has no interest in the residuary estate of the deceased.

(7) Or.59 R.51 (Edo) 2018; Or.55 R.51 (Delta) and Or.57 R.14 (Lagos), supra.

(8) Or.59 R.63 (Edo); Or.55 R.63 (Delta) 2009 and Or.60 R.16 (Lagos), supra.

(9) Ibid.

(10) With the consent of the co-applicant(s).

(11) By obtaining Certificate for Further Security.

(12) Garner, B .A., " Black's Law Dictionary", supra pg. 42

(13) Or.59 R. 64 (Edo) 2018 and Or.55 R.64 (Delta) 2009, supra.

(14) Or.59 R.67 (Edo) 2018; Or.55 R.67 (Delta) 2009 and Or.59 R.16 (Lagos). NOTE: A Motion is a written or oral application requesting a court to make a specified ruling or order.

(15) Section 28(1) AEL (Bendel) 1976, supra.

(16) "Intestacy" means the state or condition of a person who has died without a valid Will.

(17) Reimbursed for any loss suffered during the Administration of such a deceased's estate.

(18) Or.58 R.35 & R.36 (Edo) 2018; Or.54 R.35 & R.36 (Delta) 2009 and Or.59 R.8 (Lagos) 2012, supra. NOTE: Under the Lagos Rules, filing of account is at intervals not exceeding Twelve (12) Months.

(19) Or.58 R.39 (Edo) 2018; Or.54 R.39 (Delta) 2009and Or.59 R.11(1) (Lagos) 2012, supra. NOTE: The consent of the Magistrate or the Administrative Officer (of another Local Government) must first be obtained.

(20) Or.58 R.40 (Edo) 2018; Or.54 R.40 (Delta) 2009 and Or.59 R. 11(2) (Lagos) 2012, supra. "Leave of Court" is a judicial permission to follow a non-route procedure.

(21) Or.59 R.48 (Edo) 2018; Or.55 R.48 (Delta) 2009 and Or.57 R.11 (Lagos) 2012, supra.

(22) Or.59 R.49(1) (Edo) 2018; Or.55 R.49(1) (Delta) 2009 and Or.57 R.12(1) (Lagos) 2012, supra.

(23) Or.59 R.51(1) (Edo) 2018; Or.55 R.51(1) (Delta) 2009 and Or.57 R.14(1) (Lagos) 2012, supra.

(24) See the cases of Ademola V. Probate Registrar (1971) All NLR p. 155 and Erewa V. Idehen (1971)ALL NLR p. 192.

(25) A Devisee or Legatee is a recipient of property by Will.

(26) See section 26(1) AEL (Bendel) 1976, supra.

(27) See section 26(1)(b), ibid. See also Or.58 R.37 (Edo) 2018; Or.54 R.37 (Delta) 2009 and Or.59 R.6 (Lagos) 2012, supra.

(28) See Garner, B. A., "Black's Law Dictionary", supra pg.49.

(29) Ibid.

(30) Ibid pg.50. NOTE: Estate Residue is the left over estate after a part has been disposed of.

(31) Section 27(1) AEL (Bendel) 1976, supra.

CHAPTER EIGHTEEN

ADDITION AND SUBSTITUTION OF PERSONAL REPRESENTATIVE TO GRANT

ADDITION OF PERSONAL REPRESENTATIVE

An application to add personal representative who were not originally in the Grant made or initially involved in the process of obtaining Grant can be made to the Registrar.

PROCEDURE FOR ADDITIONAL PERSONAL REPRESENTATIVE

The application for Additional Applicant or Joinder of Administrator is usually supported by an affidavit sworn to by the Applicant and the consent of the person proposed to be joined must be obtained.(1) This application can also be made by a person who initially was not involved either as an Applicant or Administrator but have equal or prior right to the grant sought and desire to exercise such right. However, the Applicants or Administrators to grant cannot exceed four.(2)

Thus:

> *"(1) An application to add a personal representative, shall be made to the Registrar and shall be supported by an affidavit by the applicant, the consent of the person proposed to be added as personal representative and such other evidence as the Registrar may require.*
>
> *(2) On any such application, the Registrar may direct that a note shall be made on the original grant, of the addition of a further personal representative, or he may impound or revoke the grant or make*

such other as the circumstances of the case may require." (3)

Therefore, application for additional Personal Representative or joinder of Administrator can be made before or after obtaining grant. Once such application is approved by the Registrar, necessary forms are issued to Applicant for completion, execution and oath purposes. Soon after the payment of oath and filing fees, entries are made on the relevant forms to reflect the additional representative and if Grant has been obtained, the Grant would be amended accordingly.

REASONS FOR ADDITIONAL PERSONAL REPRESENTATIVE

An application for Additional Representative or Joinder of Administrator may arise under the following circumstances:

i. Mis-Representation Of Fact By Applicant Or Administrator
   This is where the initial Applicants or Administrators did not fully disclose the number of women (gates) who gave birth to the deceased's children or how many men, a female deceased person had her children for.
ii. Exercising Right To Grant
   Where a person having an equal or prior right over the Applicants to the grant sought, becomes aware of such right and apply to exercise same.
iii. Deceased's Infant Children Attaining Majority (4)
   Where minor children of the deceased have come of age and seek to be part of the Administration of the deceased's estate, especially where deceased's relations are the Applicants or Administrators.

iv. Lack Of Trust

Where persons beneficially interested in the estate of the deceased wish to secure their interest due to lack of trust in the present Applicants or Administrators.

v. Court Order

The Court may, on its own Motion *(Suo Motu)* or upon the application of person interested in a deceased estate appoint administrator, such person appointed can apply to be joined as an Additional Representative.

By the Operation of Law, the Statutory provision conferring power on the Court to appoint new Trust does not give power to appoint an Executor. It is important to know that the appointment of Executor is not a creation of the Law but a private one of trust and the exclusive preserve of the Testator of a Will. Thus, the Court can only appoint an Executor to replace or in addition to a proving Executor, if the terms of the Will so allow.[(5)]

SUBSTITUTION OF PERSONAL REPRESENTATIVE

In Probate matters, Substitution of Personal Representative occurs where a person is made to act or serve in place of another and can be done before or after obtaining grant. In other words, Substitution of Personal Representative arises where an Applicant has the need to substitute either of the following, due to unforeseen circumstances or exigencies:

1. Himself
2. A co-Applicant
3. A co-Administrator

REASONS FOR SUBSTITUTION OF PERSONAL REPRESENTATIVE

There are various reasons why an Applicant or Administrator may desire to bring on board a substitute for proper and effective Administration of the estate of the deceased. Some of these reasons include the following:

i. The Death Of A Co-Applicant Or Co-Administrator
   The death of a co-Applicant or co-Administrator is the most commonest reason for Substitution of Personal Representative.
   However in grant of Probate, the death of a co-Executor does not necessitate Substitution. The surviving Executor can administer the Testator's estate without the dead Executor. But where there is no surviving Executor, there is need for Substitution in order for the Administration of the Testator's estate not to be in abeyance.[6]

ii. Where a Co-Applicant or Co-Administrator travelled Outside the Country or Has Become a Resident of Another Country.
   It is important to note that in grant of Probate, with due notice to the other Executors, if any, an Executor residing outside the Country can give Power of Attorney to another to take his place.[7] But where an Executor who travelled or reside outside the Country, negate to act as Executor or give Power of Attorney to another, after being summon to prove the Will, the Executor residing within the Country can apply to administer the Testator's estate in the absence of the said Executor.

Thus:

> *"Where Probate is granted to one or some of two or more persons named as executors, whether or not power is reserved to the other or others to prove, all the powers which are by law conferred on the personal representative may be exercised by the proving executor or executors for the time being and shall be as effectual as if all the persons named as executors are concurred therein."*[(8)]

iii. Deceased's Infant Children Attaining Majority

Where a valid Will exist, such clause must be inserted in the Testator's Will.

iv. Where a Co-Applicant or Administrator Becomes Uninterested in the Process of Obtaining Grant or Acting as an Administrator in the Deceased's Estate, Due to Personal Reasons.

In grant of Probate, it is pertinent to note that, where a person named as an Executor in a Will is not interested in the process of proving the Will or acting as an Executor, such a person is entitled to renounce his Executorship.[(9)]

v. Where a co-Applicant or Administrator Becomes Incapacitated to Act as Applicant or Administrator Due to Mental or Physical Incapacity.

In grant of Probate, mental or physical incapacitation of a co-Executor does not necessitate Substitution. However, where the person so incapacitated is a sole or the only surviving proving Executor, there is need for Substitution.

PROCEDURE FOR SUBSTITUION OF PERSONAL REPRESENTATIVE

An Applicant who desire to substitute himself, a Co-Applicant or co- Administrator, must apply to the Registrar in person or through the legal representative of the deceased's estate, requesting for Authorization to Substitute. This application is usually supported by affidavit sworn to by the applicant, stating the reasons for the said Substitution. The intended substitute or suggested replacement must equally sworn to an Affidavit of Consent which is also attached to the application.

In grant of Probate where a Testator inserted a clause in his Will that a particular child of his will become an Executor once he is of age, the temporary Executor or the child mentioned in the Will who has come of age can apply to the Registrar to effect such Substitution.

Once the application is granted and the intended substitute is approved by the Registrar, the Applicant is made to pay oath and filing fees for the Substitution and thereafter the substitute will sign on the relevant Probate forms, if grant is yet to be made Where a grant has already been obtained, certain Probate forms are issued and applicant will pay necessary fees and thereafter, Certificate of Substitution is issued.

Where there is a valid Will and Probate has been granted, Applicant can only apply to substitute after obtaining Certificate of Authorization to Substitute dead Executors. Once Certificate of Authorization to Substitute has been granted, applicant can then apply for substitution. After the payment of relevant fee, substitution is effected and Certificate of Substitution is issued.

INTENDED SUBSTITUTE

In considering application for substitution in grant of Administration, the names and the relationship with the deceased, of persons on the Declaration as to Next-of-Kin form filed at the Registry play a vital role. Thus, the intended substitute or suggested replacements are usually persons earlier listed on the Declaration as to Next-of-Kin form filed. Hardly can an intended substitute emanate from oblivion. It is important to note that intended substitute must file Affidavit of Consent.

However, in grant of Probate, an Executor residing outside the Country or who travelled outside the Country can give Power of Attorney to any person to represent him, provided due notice is given to the other Executors, if any.

REFERENCES

(1) Through Affidavit of Consent. This is the case where such application is made by an existing Applicant or Administrator.

(2) See section 24(1) AEL (Bendel) 1976, supra.

(3) Or.59 R.43 & R.42 (Edo) 2018; Or.55 R.43 & R.42 (Delta) 2009 and Or.59 R.12 & R.14 (Lagos) 2012, supra.

(4) "Majority" is the status of one who has attained the age (usually 18) at which one is entitled to full civic rights and considered legally capable of handling one's own affairs- see Garner, B.A., "Black's Law Dictionary", supra pg. 1040.

(5) See Mosanya, J. A., "Common Form Probate Business", supra, pg. 178

(6) In such circumstances, applicant must apply and obtain Certificate of Authorization to Substitute, that is, leave of Court or Registrar to substitute dead Executors.

(7) See the Proviso to Or.59 R.48(1) (Edo) 2018; Or.55 R.48(1) (Delta) 2009 and Or.57 R.11(1) (Lagos) 2012, supra.

(8) Section 9(1) AEL (Bendel) 1976, supra.

(9) Or.58 R.7& Or.59 R.4 (Edo) 2018; Or.54 R.7 & Or.59 R.4 (Delta) 2009 and Or.58 R.18 (Lagos) 2012, supra. See also section 23 AEL (Bendel) 1976, supra.

CHAPTER NINETEEN

RESEALING OF GRANT AND ADDITIONAL ASSETS

RESEALING OF GRANT

The Administrator or Executor of a deceased, who before his death had lived in various States or Countries and had properties in those places,[1] can apply to the Registrar for the Resealing of Grant earlier obtained in another State or Country.

Thus, Resealing simply means to reseal with the seal of a Court, the Probate or Letters of Administration already granted in respect of the estate of the deceased, either by a Court having jurisdiction in matters of Probate in a Commonwealth Country [2] or by a High Court of another State. This process is necessary because a grant obtained in one State or Country in respect of a deceased's estate in that State or Country cannot have the operational force in respect of the deceased's estate in another State or Country.

PROCEDURE FOR RESEALING OF GRANT

Application for the Resealing of Grant can be made by the Administrator or Executor to whom the grant was made or by any person authorized in writing to apply on his behalf. [3]The following documents are attached to such application:

i. Two Certified True Copies of the grant;
ii. Two Certified True Copies of the Will Probated;[4]
iii. A power of Attorney or Letter of Authorization.[5]

Immediately the Application for Resealing is approved by the Registrar, the relevant forms are issued to Applicant for completion and thereafter return same with the prescribed filing and publication fees. [6]At the expiration of the legal notice and the gross value of the estate to be resealed having been ascertain by the Registrar, estate fee is assessed and payment called for.

Upon payment of the estate fee by the Administrator or Executor, Minute and Order is drawn up in the Order Book praying the Honourable, the Chief Judge to grant an Order to Reseal the grant earlier obtained in another State or Country. After the Order has been granted, Resealing Certificate is prepared and signed by the Registrar. The Resealing Certificate together with a Certified True Copy of the Grant is issued to the Administrator or Executor. In grant with Will annexed, a Certified True Copy of the Will Probated is also attached.

It is pertinent to note that the Registrar may not require Sureties, except where he considers that there are "special circumstances" making it desirable to do so. Also, no Limited or Temporary grant can be resealed, except by leave of the Registrar.(7)

ADDITIONAL ASSETS

The Administrator or Executor who had earlier obtained Grant can apply to the Registrar, in order to obtain a Certificate for Further Security in respect of Additional Assets that were not administered in the earlier grant made to them. This process is usually the case where the earlier grant tend to reflect part and not the totality of a deceased's estate.

REASONS FOR CERTIFICATE FOR FURTHER SECURITY

Application for Certificate for Further Security may arise under the following circumstances:

i. Where assets that were although within the knowledge of Administrators or Executors, but due to lack or insufficient proof of the continuous existence or uncertainty as to the where about of same, could not form part of the deceased's estate at the time of obtaining grant.

ii. The discovery of assets owned by the deceased which were not within the knowledge of the Administrator or Executor as at the time grant was made to them.

iii. Where the Additional Asset was a subject matter in a pending suit at the time the grant was obtained.

PROCEDURE FOR CERTIFICATE FOR FURTHER SECURITY

Any application for further security must be supported by an affidavit, stating the reasons why the additional asset was not declared in the inventory form filed in the earlier grant.(8) The application is either made by the Administrator, Executor or the Legal representative of the deceased's estate. As soon as the application is approved, relevant forms are issued, filled, filed and thereafter Certificate for Further Security is issued to the Administrators or Executors, upon payment of estate fee for the value of the Additional Asset.

It is important to note that, in some Probate matters, applicant for further security may have the need to first apply for substitution of a co-Administrator before applying and obtaining Certificate for Further Security. This is often the case where a co-Administrator in the earlier grant is indisposed to proceed with the Applicant for further security, either due to physical or mental incapacity, residency outside the country or lack of interest in acting as Administrator. Immediately the substitution is approved and effected, application for further security can then be made and proceeded with.

GRANTING OF CERTIFICATE FOR FURTHER SECURITY TO PERSONS OTHER THAN THE ADMINISTRATOR OR EXECUTOR NAMED IN A GRANT

In order for a deceased's estate not to be in abeyance and for continuity and effective Administration of such estate, persons other than the Administrator or Executor named in a Grant in respect of a deceased's estate are allowed to substitute and obtain Certificate for Further Security where there are no surviving Administrators or proving Executors.

Applicants for further security under such circumstances must apply and obtain Certificate of Authorization to substitute the dead Administrators or Executors before applying and obtaining Certificate for Further Security for the Additional Asset.

PROCEDURE FOR CERTIFICATE OF AUTHORIZATION TO SUBSTITUTE

In order to obtain authority to administer in place of dead Administrators or Executors, Applicant must apply to the Registrar for authority to substitute. The following are documents attached to such application:

i. Affidavit of Substitution sworn by Applicant;
ii. Affidavit of Consent sworn by Co-Applicant;[9]
iii. Certified True Copies of Death Certificates of Administrators or Executors.[10]
iv. Letter of Authorization given by other children of the deceased or beneficially interested persons in the deceased's estate.[11]

Immediately the application for authority to substitute is approved, relevant forms are issued, filled and filed. In other to erase possible deception, such applications are usually published.[(12)] However, no second set of probate form process is required.

After the expiration of the Legal Notice, and payment of a paltry sum for certification, Certificate of Authorization to Substitute is issued. Upon issuance of this Certificate, Applicants can then apply for Certificate for Further Security and the procedure for obtaining Certificate for Further Security is duly observed.

REFERENCES

(1) Personal property and/or real property.

(2) A group of Countries that have chosen to be politically linked.

(3) Or.59 R.55(1) (Edo) 2018; Or.55 R.55(1) (Delta) 2009 and Or.58 R26(1) (Lagos) 2012, supra.

(4) Or.59 R.55(6) ibid; Or.55 R.55(6) ibid and Or.58 R.26(6) ibid.

(5) Where an agent or someone else apply on behalf of the Administrator or Executor. See Or.59 R.55(1) ibid; Or.55 R.55(1) ibid and Or.58 R.26(1) ibid.

(6) Relevant forms for Resealing include: the Forwarding Letter, Application for Resealing, Inventory, Oath for Resealing and Bank Certificate (if necessary). NOTE: Single Publication is usually required - see Or.59 R.55(2)(b) ibid; Or.55 R.55(2)(b) ibid and Or.58 R.(26)(2)(b) ibid.

(7) Or.59 R.55(3)(5) ibid; Or.55 R.55(3)(5) ibid and Or.58 R.26(2)(b) ibid. See Appendix 47 for specimen of Resealing Certificate.

(8) The Additional Asset could be Money in Bank, Shares, Pension, Gratuity, Real Property, Fund with Pension Managers, etc.

(9) The Co-Applicant must express willingness to act as a co-Administrator.

(10) In the absence of a death certificate, Affidavit of Death can suffice.

(11) Authorizing or nominating the Applicants as replacement for the dead Administrators or Executors.

(12) Publication can be multiple or single, depending on the circumstances of each particular case.

CHAPTER TWENTY

AFFIDAVITS IN PROBATE MATTERS

THE NATURE AND FEATURES OF AFFIDAVITS

Affidavit play vital role in Probate matters and its importance cannot be over emphasized. Affidavit is a written statement of facts sworn on Oath to be true. In other words, it is a voluntary declaration of facts written down and sworn to by the declarant before an officer authorized to administer Oaths.(1) A person who sworn to an affidavit is called a Declarant or a Deponent.

Every affidavit used in non-contentious Probate business shall satisfy the requirements of the Evidence Act on affidavits.(2)Under the Evidence Act, 2011, a written declaration of facts must meet certain requirements for it to be a valid affidavit met for court purposes and some of these requirements include the following:

i. The contents of affidavits must be statement believe to be true

> *"Every affidavit used in court shall contain only a statement of facts and circumstances to which the witness deposes, either of his own personal knowledge or from information which he believes to be true."(3)*

It is important to note that, when a person deposes to his belief in any matter of fact, and his belief is derived from any source other than his own personal knowledge, he must set forth explicitly the facts and circumstances forming the ground, of his belief and when such belief is derived from information received from other person, the name of his informant must be stated and reasonable particulars must be given in respect of the informant, the time, place and circumstance of the information.[4]

ii. Affidavit must be filed

> *"Before an affidavit is used in the court for any purpose, the original shall be filed in the court, and the original or an office copy shall alone be recognized for any purpose in the court."*[5]

In Probate matters, for any affidavit to be acted upon, it must be filed at the Probate Registry.

iii. Affidavits must be sworn before a person duly authorized

> *"Any affidavit sworn before any Judge, officer or other person duly authorized to take affidavits in Nigeria may be used in court in all cases where affidavits are admissible."*[6]

Similarly;

> *"Unless the Registrar otherwise directs, every oath, affidavit or guarantee required of a personal application shall be sworn or executed by all the deponents or sureties before an authorized officer."*[7]

It is of great importance to note that, it is the swearing that makes a document an affidavit and where the document is not sworn to, it is only a piece of paper, not an affidavit.[8]

Thus:

> *"Every application for a grant shall be supported by an oath in the form applicable to the circumstances of the case, which shall be contained in any affidavit sworn by the applicant and by such other persons as the Registrar may require."*[(9)]

Sections 117 to 120 of the Evidence Act (2011), analyzed the features of affidavit to be observed by persons before whom affidavits are sworn. Although, affidavits are documentary evidence, but in every case where proof is allowed to be by affidavit, the Court may require the personal attendance of the deponent to appear and be examined orally in respect of his affidavit and this examination may take place before any affidavit has been sworn or prepared.[(10)]

THE USES OF AFFIDAVITS IN PROBATE MATTERS

Apart from affidavits being required by the Registrar from persons he may deem fit for the purpose of satisfying himself as to due execution, terms, conditions, date of execution of Wills, affidavits can be used for the following purposes:

i. To correct wrong spellings in names, either of the Deceased, Applicant, Administrator or Executor. This occurs where the deceased's name is wrongly spelt on the death certificate or where the Applicant, Administrator or Executor name is wrongly spelt on their means of identification.
ii. To include additional name to that of the Deceased, Applicant, Administrator or Executor. This occur where it is necessary to describe the Deceased,

Applicant, Administrator or Executor in a grant by some name in addition to his true name.[11]

iii. To correct wrong date of death inserted in a deceased's death certificate.

iv. To correct wrong place of death inserted in a deceased's death certificate.

v. To show that a warning was duly served on a Caveator and the person warning has not received summons for direction.[12]

vi. To show particulars of contrary interest which a Caveator may have in a deceased's estate, at the instance of any person interested in the estate. [13]

vii. To show that a person cited who is willing to accept or take grant has not been served by the Citor's notice of application for grant.[14]

viii. For giving expert evidence of foreign law in respect of any application for grant.

Thus:

> *"Where evidence as to law of any Country or territory outside the State is required on any application for a grant, the Registrar may accept an affidavit from the person whom, having regard to the particulars of his knowledge or experience given in the affidavit, he regards as suitably qualified to give expert evidence of the Law in question."*[15]

ix. To attest the authenticity and genuineness of content of documents, signatures, terms and conditions etc for example;

(a) For proof that the terms and conditions of a valid Will was duly observed.

Thus:

> *"The Registrar may require an affidavit from any person he may think fit, for the purpose of satisfying himself as to any of the matters referred to in rules 15, 16 and 17 and in any such affidavit sworn by an attesting witness or other person present at the time of the execution of Will, the deponent shall depose to the manner in which the Will was executed."*(16)

(b) For proof of execution where attestation clause in a Will is defective.

Therefore:

> *"(1) if there is no attestation clause or if the attestation clause is Insufficient, the court shall require an affidavit from at least one of the subscribing witnesses, if either of them is living, to prove that the Will was, in fact executed in accordance with those enactments.*
>
> *(2) The affidavit shall be engrossed and form part of the probate, so that the probate may be a complete document on the face of it."*(17)

(c) For proof that interlineations, alteration erasures or obliterations existed in a Will before its execution.

Thus:

> *"Where interlineations, alterations, erasures, or obliterations appear in the Will (unless duly executed or recited in or otherwise identified by the attestation clause), an affidavit in proof of their having existed in the Will before its execution, shall be filed."*[(18)]

x. For supporting applications. For example, the following applications must be supported by an affidavit:

(a) Application for Substitution;
(b) Application for Additional Asset (Further Security);
(c) Application for Additional Personal Representative;[(19)]
(d) Application for Joinder of Administrator;[(20)]
(e) Application for Limited Grant;[(21)]
(f) Application for Orders in respect of Citation;[(22)]
(g) Application for Subpoena.[(23)]

TYPES OF AFFIDAVITS

There are various kinds of affidavits relating to Probate matters, some of which include the following:

i. Affidavit of Identity that is, Reconciliation of Names;
ii. Affidavit of Substitution;[(24)]
iii. Affidavit of Consent;[(25)]
iv. Affidavit of Additional Asset (Further Security);
v. Affidavit of Loss of Original Death Certificate;
vi. Affidavit of Attesting Witness of Wills;
vii. Affidavit of Death;

viii. Affidavit of Additional Personal Representative or Joinder of Administrator;

ix. Affidavit of Witness or Attestation;[26]

x. Affidavit as to due execution of Will;[27]

xi. Affidavit of Interest.[28]

xii. Affidavit to Show:[29]

(a) That warning was duly served on Caveator and no summons for direction received.

(b) That Citation was duly served and the person cited has not entered an appearance.

(c) That a person cited who is willing to accept or take a grant has not been served by Citor's notice of application for grant.

xiii. Affidavit to show cause.[30]

EFFECT OF AFFIDAVITS WHEN ALLOWED AS PROOF

A great deal of evidence is submitted by affidavit. In Probate matters, affidavits tend to include facts, cure or correct defects, resolve and reconcile discrepancies observed in documents, Wills, means of identification [31], death certificate and show compliance with procedures etc. Thus, where proof is allowed to be by affidavit, the general effect are as follows:

i. To introduce and include facts or circumstances not initially on board. For example, Affidavit of Additional Personal Representative or joinder of Administrator, Affidavit of Additional Asset, Affidavit of Substitution, etc

ii. To correct and cure defects observed in documents, Wills etc. for example, Affidavit as to due execution, terms, conditions, date of execution of Will.

iii. To resolve and reconcile any discrepancies in documents, death certificate, means of identification, etc. For example, Affidavit of Identity, place of death, date of death, etc.

iv. To show compliance with the practice and procedures of certain rules and obligations. For example, Affidavit to show cause, Affidavit in support of application, etc.

REFERENCES

(1) See Garner, B. A., "Black's Law Dictionary", supra pg.66.

(2) Or.59 R.76 (Edo) 2018 and Or.55 R.76 (Delta) 2009, supra.

(3) Section 115(1) Evidence Act, 2011.

(4) Section 115(3)(4) ibid. In affidavit, facts of personal knowledge must be distinguished from the other facts- see the case of Markus Natina Gundiri & Anor. V. Rear Admiral M. H. Nyako (2012) MRSCJ Vol. iii p.169.

(5) Section 108 ibid.

(6) Section 109 ibid. Also see the case of Osasuyi V. Mudashiru (2013) 26 WRN P. 189.

(7) Or.59 R.8(7) (Edo) 2018; Or.55 R.8(7) (Delta) 2009 and Or.57 R.3(7) (Lagos) 2012, supra.

(8) See the case of Osasuyi V. Mudashiru (2013), supra.

(9) Or.59 R.10(1) (Edo) 2018; Or.55 R.10(1) (Delta) 2009 and Or.57 R.6(1) (Lagos) 2012,supra.

(10) Or.59 R.40 (Edo) 2018 and Or.55 R.40 (Delta) 2009. See the cases of Ndule V. Ojiakor (2013) and Odutola V. Mabogunje (2013), supra.

(11) Or.59 R.11 (Edo) 2018; Or.55 R.11 (Delta) 2009 and Or.57 R.7 (Lagos) 2012, supra.

(12) Or.59 R.57(11) (Edo) 2018; Or.55 R.57(11) (Delta) 2009 and Or.59 R.18(12) (Lagos) 2012, supra.

(13) Known as Affidavit of Interest. See Or.59 R.57(7) (Edo) 2018; Or.55 R.57(7) (Delta) 2009 and Or.59 R.18(8) (Lagos} 2012, supra.

(14) Or.59 R.59(4) (Edo) 2018; Or.55 R.59(4) (Delta) 2009 and Or.58 R.28(4) (Lagos) 2012, supra.

(15) Or.59 R.20 (Edo) 2018; Or,55 R.20 (Delta) 2009 and Or.57 R.18 (Lagos) 2012, supra.

(16) Or.59 R.18 (Edo) 2018; Or.55 R.18 (Delta) 2009 and Or.58 R.9 (Lagos) 2012, supra.

(17) Or.58 R.20 (Edo)2018; Or.54 R.20 (Delta) 2009 and Or.58 R.5 (Lagos) 2012, supra.

(18) Or.58 R.24(3) & Or.59 R.36 (Edo) 2018; Or.54 R.24(3) & Or.55 R.36 (Delta) 2009 and Or.58 R.11(3) (Lagos) 2012, supra.

(19) Or.59 R.43(1) (Edo) 2018; Or.55 R.43(1) (Delta) 2009 and Or.59 R.12(1) (Lagos) 2012, supra.

(20) Or.59 R.42 (Edo) 2018; Or.55 R.42 (Delta) 2009 and Or.59 R.14 (Lagos) 2012, supra.

(21) Or.59 R.63 (Edo) 2018; Or.55 R.63 (Delta) and Or.60 R.16 (Lagos) 2012, supra.

(22) Or. 59 R.59(5)(6) (Edo) 2018; Or.55 R.59(5)(6) (Delta) 2009 and Or.58 R.28(5)(6) (Lagos) 2012, supra.

(23) Or.59 R.62(2) (Edo) 2018; Or.55 R.62(2) (Delta) 2009 and Or.60 R.15(2) (Lagos) 2012, supra.

(24) Sworn to by Applicant or Administrator who intend to substitute.

(25) Sworn to by the person expressing willingness to become co-Applicant or co-Administrator.

(26) Sworn to by an Applicant submitting the reply to Notice of Application on behalf of persons served.

(27) Or.58 R.20 (Edo) 2018; Or.54 R.20 (Delta) 2009 and Or.58 R.5 (Lagos) 2012, supra.

(28) Or.59 R.57(7) (Edo) 2018; Or.55 R.57(7) (Delta) 2009 and Or.59 R.18(8) (Lagos) 2012, supra.

(29) Or.59 R.57(11), R.59(4)(6) (Edo) 2018; Or.55 R.57(11), R.59(4)(6) (Delta) 2009 and Or.59 R.18(12) & Or.58 R.28(4)(6) (Lagos} 2012, supra.

(30) Or.58 R.41(4) (Edo) 2018; Or.54 R.41(4) (Delta) 2009 and Or.57 R.16(5) (Lagos) 2012, supra.

(31) Means of identification may include International Passport, Driver's Licence, Voter's Card, ATM Card, National identification Card. Etc.

CHAPTER TWENTY ONE

SEARCHES AND CERTIFICATION OF PROBATE DOCUMENTS

Probate Documents are public documents open for public inspection. Public documents are documents forming the official acts or records of the official acts of:

i. The Sovereign Authority;
ii. Official bodies and Tribunals;
iii. Public Officers, Legislative, Judicial or Executive, whether of Nigeria or elsewhere;
iv. Public Records kept in Nigeria of private documents.[(1)]

SEARCHES IN PROBATE MATTERS

A search in Probate matter may be liken to Zone Search, which is the examination of public documents or records for information.[(2)] Probate documents being a public document, any interested person who desire to know or seek information regarding a particular estate of which grant of Probate or Letters of Administration has been granted, yet to be granted or the issue as to whether or not a deceased left a Will, can do so by conducting a search at the Registry.

Thus:

"(1) Every original Will, of which probate or administration with Will annexed is granted, shall be filed and kept in the probate registry, in such manner as to secure at once the due preservation and convenient inspection of same.

(2) *A copy of every such Will, and of the probate or administration, shall be preserved in a book kept for the purpose in the registry."*[(3)]

Similarly,

> *"All original Wills and other documents which are under the control of the court shall be deposited and preserved in such a place as the Chief Justice may direct and any Wills or other documents so deposited shall, subject to the control of the court and the provision of probate rules and orders, be open to inspection."*[(4)]

PROCEDURE FOR CONDUCTING SEARCHES IN PROBATE MATTERS

A person who intends to conduct a search on the estate of a deceased must apply to the Registrar. Such application can be made personally or through legal representative and must contain the following information:

i. The name of the deceased;
ii. The date of death;
iii. The relationship between the applicant and deceased;
iv. The purpose or reason for the search.

Once the application is approved by the Registrar and the prescribed fees paid, Applicant is then permitted to search through the deceased's estate file in the presence of an authorized officer. Where the purpose of a search is to ascertain whether or not a deceased left a Will, a designated officer of the Registry usually conduct the search and thereafter, on behalf of the Registrar, furnish the Applicant with the search report.

CERTIFICATION OF PROBATE DOCUMENTS

Certification is the act of attesting while to certify means to authenticate or verify in writing, to attest as being true or as meeting certain criteria.[5]

It is the duty of every public officer having the custody of a public document which any person has a right to inspect, to give to that person on demand, a copy of it on payment of the prescribed fees with a certificate written at the foot of such copy that it is a true copy of such document or part thereof and the certificate must be dated and subscribed by the officer with his name, official title and must be sealed, whenever such officer is authorized by law to make use of seal.[6]The copies of such documents so certified are referred to as Certified True Copies and such Certified True Copies can be produced in proof of the contents of the public documents or parts of the public documents of which they purport to be copies.[7]

Therefore:

> *"An official copy of the whole or any part of a Will or an official certificate of any grant of administration may, on payment of the fee prescribed by probate rules and orders, be obtained from the probate registry."*[8]

It is important to know that the Original Will cannot be given out for any purpose without the direction in writing of the Court where the Will is lodged, however, a certified transcript, under the seal of the Court of the Probate or Administration with the Will annexed, may be obtained from the Court.[9] In other words, Certified True Copies of Probate Documents are made available on demand and upon payment of the prescribed fees to interested persons.

PROCEDURE FOR OBTAINING CERTIFIED TRUE COPY OF PROBATE DOCUMENTS

A person interested in obtaining a Certified True Copy of any Probate document, must apply to the Registrar, either in person or through a legal representative. Such application must contain among other things:

i. The name of the deceased;
ii. The tile of the document;
iii. The number of copies to be certified.

Upon the approval of the application and payment of the prescribed fees, the said document is certified by an authorized officer of the Registry in accordance with the provisions relating to certification of document, to wit:

"(1) .... a certificate written at the foot of such copy that it is a true copy of such document or part of it as the case may be.

(2) ....shall be dated and subscribed by such officer with his name and his official title, and shall be sealed, whenever such officer is authorized by law to make use of a seal, and such copies so certified shall be called certified copies."(10)

It is of importance to know that Probate documents requiring certification can either be:

(1) Copies of original documents or Photostat of office copies filed or deposited in the Registry.

Thus:

"Where copies are required of original Wills or other documents deposited under

the provisions of any written law, such copies may be photostat copies sealed with the seal of the registry and issued as office copies and, where such office copies are available, copies certified under the hand of a Registrar to be true copies shall be issued only if it is required that the seal of the court be affixed thereto."[(11)]

OR

(2) Photostat copies of original documents in possession of the applicant which are usually attached to application for certified true copy. Therefore, where copies to be certified emanate from the applicant, such copies are examined vis-à-vis the office copies of the documents of which they purport to be copies, before certification.[(12)]

It is pertinent to note that searches can be conducted in Probate matters and Certified True Copies of Probate Documents can also be obtained, at any given time, even when there is a pending suit in respect of the deceased's estate.

REFERENCES

(1) Section 102 Evidence Act, supra. See also the case of Gov. Kwara State V. Irepodun Block Manu. Co. (2013) 12 WRN P. 145.

(2) See Garner, B. A., "Black's Law Dictionary", supra, pg.1469.

(3) Or.58 R.17 & Or.59 R.29 (Edo) 2018; Or.54 R.17 & Or.55 R.29 (Delta) 2009 and Or.58 R.2 (Lagos) 2012, supra.

(4) Section 33 AEL (Bendel) 1976, supra.

(5) Garner, B. A., "Black's Law Dictionary", supra pg. 258. See also the case of Adeyefe V. Bamgboye (2013) 19 WRN p. 14.

(6) Section 104 (1)(2) Evidence Act, supra.

(7) Section 105, ibid.

(8) Section 34 AEL (Bendel) 1976, supra.

(9) Or.58 R.18 & Or.59 R.30 (Edo) 2018; Or.54 R.18 & Or.55 R.30 (Delta) and Or.58 R.3 (Lagos) 2012, supra.

(10) Section 104 (1)(2) Evidence Act, supra. See also the case of Adeyefe V. Bamgboye (2013), supra.

(11) Or.59 R.69(1) (Edo) 2018 and Or.55 R.69(1) (Delta) 2009.

(12) Or.59 R.69(2) ibid and Or.55 R.69(2) ibid.

CHAPTER TWENTY- TWO

NOTICE OF PROHIBITION AND CAVEAT

NOTICE TO PROHIBIT GRANT

A "Notice" is a legal notification required by Law, agreement or imparted by operation of Law as a result of some facts, while "prohibition" is a law or order that forbids a certain action.[(1)]

Thus, a Notice to prohibit grant is an official appeal forbidding the Registrar from entertaining any application for grant [(2)] or for granting Probate or Administration to some particular persons[(3)] in respect of the estate of the deceased named therein.

A Notice to Prohibit Grant may be filed in the Registry.[(4)] Therefore, any aggrieved person or person who thinks his interest in the Administration of the estate of a deceased is at risk, can file in the Registry a Notice to Prohibit grant of Probate or Letters of Administration.

EFFECT OF NOTICE TO PROHIBIT GRANT

The Probate Rules make mentioned of:

i. Notice to Prohibit grant of Administration Without Will [(5)];
ii. Notice to Prohibit grant of Probate or Administration With Will Annexed;[(6)]

In practice, Notice to Prohibit grant is mostly used in Letters of Administration Without Will. Once the Notice is filed, all actions in respect of granting Probate or Letters of Administration in the estate of a deceased are stayed. However, the effect of Notice to Prohibit grant of Probate or Letters of Administration are the same, namely:

i. A notice to prohibit grant remain in force for three months from the day of filing but may be renewed from time to time.

ii. A notice to prohibit grant does not affect a grant made on the day on which the notice is filed.

iii. The person filing the notice must be warned in writing delivered at the place mentioned in the notice as his address.

iv. Notices in the nature of citation must be given in such manner as the Court directs.(7)

CAVEAT

A Caveat simply means "WARNING". In other words, it is a formal notice or warning given by a party to a Court or Court Officer requesting a suspension of proceedings or action.

A Caveat against a grant of Probate or Letters of Administration must be filed in the Registry and it is mostly used in Will contest. A Caveator is one who files a Caveat, especially to challenge the validity of a Will while the Caveatee is one whose interest is challenged by a Caveat.

Thus:

> *"Any person who wishes to ensure that no grant is sealed without Notice to himself, may enter a caveat in the registry."(8)*

Once a Caveat is filed, all actions on application for grant of Probate or Letters of Administration are stayed.

PROCEDURE FOR CAVEAT AND ITS EFFECT

The following are the required procedure and general effect of Caveat:

(1) Any person who wishes to enter a caveat may do so by:

Completing civil form53in the appropriate book at the Registry and obtaining an acknowledgment copy from the authorized officer;

OR

Sending through the post at his own risk, a notice in form 51 to the Registry in which he wishes the caveat to be entered.[9]

(2) Where a caveat is entered by a Legal Practitioner on the Caveator's behalf, the name of the Caveator must be stated.[10]

(3) It is the duty of the Registrar to maintain a register of caveats entered in the Registry and on receiving an application for a grant, he must cause such register to be searched and notify the applicant in the event of a caveat having been entered against the sealing of a grant for which application has been made.[11]

(4) A caveat remains in force for six months from the date on which it is entered and then ceases to have effect without prejudice to the entry or renewal of a further caveat. [12] Thus the Register will not allow any grant to be sealed if he has knowledge of an effective caveat in respect of a deceased's estate. However, a caveat does not affect a grant made on the day which the caveat is entered.[13]

(5) A Caveator may be warned or served with a warning notice by the Registrar, at the instance of any person interested in the deceased's estate, requesting the Caveator to give particulars of any contrary interest which he may have in the estate.[14]

(6) A Caveator who has not entered an appearance to a warning, may at anytime withdraw his caveat by giving notice at the Registry and the caveat shall thereupon

cease to have effect and if he has been warned, the Caveator must give notice of withdrawal of the caveat to the person warning.[(15)]

(7) A Caveator having an interest contrary to that of the person warning may within eight days of service of the warning upon him, inclusive of the day of such service or at any time thereafter, if no affidavit showing that the warning was duly served has been filed, enter an appearance in the Registry and make an entry in the appropriate book and thereafter be served on the person warning.[(16)]

(8) A Caveator having no interest contrary to that of the person warning but wish to show cause against the sealing of a grant may, within eight days of service of the warning upon him, inclusive of the day of such service or at anytime thereafter, if no affidavit showing that the warning was duly served has been filed by the person warning, issue and serve summons for directions which must be returnable before the Registrar.[(17)]

(9) If the time limited for appearance has expired and the Caveator has not entered an appearance, the person warning may file in the Registry, an affidavit showing that the warning was duly served and that he has not received summons for directions and thereupon the caveat shall cease to have effect.[(18)]

(10) Any caveat in respect of which an appearance to a warning has been entered must remain in force until the commencement of a Probate action, unless the Registrar otherwise direct.[(19)]

(11) No further caveat may be entered by or on behalf of any Caveator whose caveat has ceased to have effect under

sub-rule(11) or (13) of rule 57 Order 59, except with the leave of the Registrar.[20]

(12) Upon the commencement of a Probate action, the Registrar must, in respect of each caveat then in force, other than a caveat entered by the claimant, give to the Caveator notice of the commencement of the action and upon the subsequent entry of a caveat at any time when the action is pending, shall likewise notify the Caveator of the existence of the action.[21]

(13) Unless the Registrar otherwise directs:

(i) Any caveat in force at the commencement of proceedings by way of citation or motion shall unless withdrawn remain in force until an application for a grant is made by the person shown to be entitled thereto by the decision of the Court in such proceedings and upon such application, any caveat entered by a party who had notice of the proceedings shall cease to have effect.[22]

(ii) The commencement of a Probate action shall, whether or not any caveat has been filed, operate to prevent the sealing of a grant until application for a grant is made by the person shown to be entitled thereto by the decision of the Court in such action and upon such application, any caveat filed by a party who had notice of the action or by a Caveator who was given notice, shall cease to have effect.[23]

REGISTRAR'S RESPONSE TO NOTICE OF PROHIBITION AND CAVEAT

When a Notice to Prohibit grant or Caveat is filed, the Registrar's immediate response is to stay all action on the application for Probate or Letters of Administration in respect of the estate of the deceased named therein, especially if the process of obtaining grant has commenced.

Thus:

"(2) A dispute between persons entitled to a grant in the same degree, shall be brought by application before the Registrar.

(3) If an application under this rule is brought before the Registrar, he shall not allow any grant to be sealed until such application is fully disposed of."[(24)]

In most cases where a notice to prohibit grant is filed in respect of the estate of a deceased in which the process of obtaining grant has already commenced, the Registrar after staying actions on the process of obtaining grant, try as much as possible to resolve the issues between the disputing parties amicably. To this effect, all the parties concerned and their counsels are by a formal letter invited to the Registry at a given time and date, for an important discussion, where all issues raised in respect of the estate of the deceased are addressed.

At such meetings, once there is an amicable settlement between the disputing parties, the decision arrived at is binding on all parties and the stay on the process of obtaining grant is lifted. However, where disputing parties are unable to reach an amicable settlement,[(25)] parties are thereby advise to seek redress in court.

It is important to note that in cases where caveats are filed, Probate Court action are usually instituted immediately.[(26)]

REFERENCES

(1) See Garner, B.A., "Black's Law Dictionary", supra pgs. 1164 and 1331 respectively.

(2) If no application has been made yet.

(3) If the process of obtaining grant has commenced.

(4) Or.58 R.13 & Or.59 R.25 (Edo) 2018; Or.54 R.13 & Or.55 R.25 (Delta) 2009 and (5 Or.59 R.18(1) (Lagos) 2012, supra.

(5) Or.58 R13, ibid and Or.54 R.13, ibid.

(6) Or.59 R.25 (Edo) 2018 and Or.55 R.25 (Delta) 2009, supra.

(7) Or.58 R.14 & Or.59 R.26 (Edo) 2018 and Or.54 R.14 & Or.55 R.26 (Delta) 2009, supra.

(8) Or.59 R.57(1) (Edo) 2018; Or.55 R.57(1) (Delta) 2009 and Or.59 R.18(2) (Lagos) 2012. See also section 21 AEL (Bendel) 1976, supra.

(9) Or.59 R.57(2) ibid; Or.55 R.57(2) and Or.59 R.18(3) ibid.

(10) Or.59 R.57(3) ibid; Or.55 R.57(3) ibid and Or.59 R.18(4) ibid.

(11) Or.59 R.57(5) ibid; Or.55 R.57(5) ibid and Or.59 R.18(6) ibid.

(12) Or.59 R.57(4) ibid; Or.55 R.57(4) ibid and Or.59 R.18(5) ibid.

(13) Or.59 R.57(6) ibid; Or.55 R.57(6) ibid and Or.59 R. 18(7) ibid.

(14) Or.59 R.57(7) ibid; Or.55 R.57(7) ibid and Or.59 R.18(8) ibid.

(15) Or.59 R.57(8) ibid Or.55 R.57(8) ibid and Or.59 R.18(10) ibid.

(16) Or.59R.57(9) ibid; Or.55 R.57(9) and Or.59 R.18(9) ibid.

(17) Or.59 R.57(10) ibid; Or.55 R.57(10) and Or.59 R.18(11) ibid.

(18) Or.59 R.57(11) ibid; Or.55 R.57(11) ibid and Or.59 R.18(12) ibid.

(19) Or.59 R.57(13) ibid; Or.55 R.57(13) and Or.59 R.18(14) ibid.

(20) Or.59 R.57(14) ibid; Or.55 R.57(14) and Or.59 R.18(15) ibid.

(21) Or.59 R.57(12) ibid; Or.55 R.57(12) ibid and Or.59 R.18(13) ibid.

(22) Or.59 R.57(13)(a) ibid; Or.55 R.57(13)(a) ibid and Or.59 R.18(14)(a) ibid.

(23) Or.59 R.57(13)(C) ibid; Or.55 R.57(13)(C) ibid and Or.59 R.18(14)(C) ibid.

(24) Or.59 R.44(2)(3) (Edo) 2018; Or.55 R.44(2)(3) (Delta) 2009 and Or.59 R.13(2)(3) (Lagos) 2012, supra.

(25) Where there is a deadlock.

(26) This is usually the case, especially in Will contest.

CHAPTER TWENTY-THREE

CITATION

MEANING OF CITATION

A Citation is a Court issued Writ that commands a person to appear at a certain time and place to do something demanded in the Writ or to show cause for not doing so.(1)In other words, Citation is a Probate process or Summon issued by the Court on its own Motion (*Suo Motu*) or upon an application by any person interested in the estate of a deceased person. The person issuing the Citation is called "the Citor" while "the person Cited" is the one being summoned.

PURPOSES FOR CITATIONS AND PROCEDURE

i. A citation to accept or refuse a grant may be issued at the instance of any person who would himself be entitled to a grant, in the event of the person cited renouncing his right thereto.(2)

ii. Where power to make a grant to an Executor has been reserved, a citation calling on him to accept or refuse a grant may be issued at the instance of the Executors who have proved the Will or the Executors of the last survivor of the deceased Executor who have proved.(3) It is pertinent to know that the rule of Executor of a sole or last surviving Executor of a Testator is the Executor of that Testator applies here.

THE RULE OF EXECUTOR OF EXECUTOR REPRESENTS ORIGINAL TESTATOR

This rule simply state that the Executor of a sole or last surviving Executor of a Testator is the Executor of that Testator, that is, Executor of Executor represents original Testator.(4) So long as the chain of such representation is unbroken, the last Executor in the chain is the last Executor of every preceding Testator.[5]

Every person in the chain of representation to a Testator has the same right in respect of the real and personal estate of that Testator as the original Executor would have had if living and is answerable to the extent to which the estate of that Testator has come to his hands, as if he were an original Executor.[6]

The chain of such representation is broken by an intestacy, the failure of a Testator to appoint an Executor or the failure to obtain Probate of a Will, but is not broken by a temporary grant of Administration if Probate is subsequently granted.[7]

However, this rule will not apply to an Executor who does not prove the Will of his Testator and in the case of Executor who on his death lives surviving him some other Executor of his Testator who afterwards proves the Will, it shall ceased to apply on such Probate been granted.[8]

(iii) A citation calling on an executor who has intermeddled in the estate of the deceased to show cause why he should not be ordered to take a grant, may be issued at the instance of any person interested in the estate at any time after the expiration of six months from the death of the deceased.[9]

(iv) A citation to propound a Will must be directed to the Executors named in the Will and to all persons interested and may be issued at the instance of any Citor having an interest contrary to that of the Executors or such other persons.[10]

A Will is being propounded when an application for Probate of the Will is lodge by the Executors with the Probate Registrar. Thus, the propounder of a Will is an Executor or Administrator who offers a Will or other testamentary document for admission to Probate.[11]

Every citation must be settled by the Registrar before being issued and every averment in a citation and such other information as the Registrar may require must be certified by an affidavit sworn to by the Citor,[12] however in special circumstances, the Registrar may accept an affidavit sworn by the Citor's legal practitioner.[13]The Citor must enter a caveat before issuing a citation and every Will referred to in a citation must be lodged in the Registry except, the Will is not in the Citor's possession and the Registrar is satisfied that it is impracticable to require it to be lodged.[14]

Citation must be served personally on the person Cited, unless the Registrar, on cause shown affidavit, directs some other mode of service which may include notice by advertisements. A person Cited to appear may within eight days of service of the citation upon him, inclusive of the day of such service or at any time thereafter, enter an appearance in the Registry [15] and If he is willing to accept or take a grant, may apply ex-parte to the Registrar for an Order for a grant on filing an affidavit showing that he has entered an appearance and that he has not been served by the Citor's notice of application for grant.[16]

However, where the time limited for appearance has expired and the person Cited has not entered an appearance, the Citor may:

(a) Apply to the Registrar for an Order for a grant to himself in the case of a citation to accept or refuse grant.[17]

(b) Apply to the Registrar for an Order that a note be made on the grant that an Executor in respect of whom power was reserved has been duly cited and has not appeared and that all his rights in respect of the Executorship have wholly ceased.[18]

(c) Apply to the Registrar by Summons which must be served on person Cited, for an Order requiring Executor who has intermeddled in the estate of the deceased to take a grant within a specified time or a grant to himself or some other person specified in the Summons.[19]

(d) Where a person Cited has entered an appearance but failed to applied for a grant or prosecute his application with reasonable diligence, the Citor may apply by Summons to the Registrar, for an Order striking out the appearance and such other Order listed in sub-rule (5) rule 59 Order 59 as the case may be.[20]

All caveats, warning, citations and appearance must contain an address for service within the Court's jurisdiction.[21]

REFERENCES

(1) Garner, B. A., "Black's Law Dictionary", supra pg. 277.

(2) Or.59 R.59(1) (Edo) 2018; Or.55 R.59(1) (Delta) 2009 and Or.58 R.28(1) (Lagos) 2012, supra.

(3) Or.59 R.59(2) ibid; Or.55 R.59(2) ibid and Or.58 R.28(2)ibid.

(4) Section 8(1) AEL (Bendel) 1976, supra.

(5) Section 8(2) ibid.

(6) Section 8(4) ibid.

(7) Section 8(3) ibid

(8) See the Proviso to section 8(1), ibid.

(9) Or.59 R.59(3) (Edo) 2018; Or.55 R.59(3) (Delta) 2009 and Or.58 R. 28(3) (Lagos) 2012, supra.

(10) OR.59 R.60(1) (Edo) 2018; Or.55 R.60(1) (Delta) 2009 and Or.58 R.29(1) (Lagos) 2012, supra.

(11) See Nsefik V. Muna (2014), supra.

(12) That is an affidavit attesting that the averment and other information in the Citation as being true.

(13) Or.59 R.58(1)(2) (Edo) 2018; Or.55 R.58(1)(2) (Delta) and Or.58 R.27(1)(2) (Lagos) 2012, supra.

(14) Or.59 R.58(3) ibid; Or.55, R.58(3)(5) ibid and Or.58 R.27(4)(6) ibid.

(15) If no application has been made by the Citor under sub-rule (5) of Rule 59 or sub-rule (2) of Rule 60, Order 59 High Court of Justice, Edo State (Civil Procedure) Rules,2018 – see Or.59 R. 58(6) ibid; Or.55 R.(4)(6) ibid and Or.58 R.27(5)(7) ibid.

(16) Or.59 R. 59(4) (Edo) 2018; Or.55 R.59(4) (Delta) 2009 and Or.58 R.28(4) (Lagos) 2012, supra.

(17) Or.59 R.59(5)(a) ibid; Or.55 R.59(5)(a) ibid and Or.58 R.28(5)(a) ibid.

(18) Or.59 R.58(5)(b) ibid; Or.55 R.59(5)(b) ibid andOr.58 R.28(5)(b) ibid.

(19) Or.59 R.59(5)(c) ibid; Or.55 R.59(5)(c) ibid and Or.58 R.28(5)(c) ibid.

(20) Or.59 R.59(7) ibid; Or.55 R.59(7) ibid and Or.58 R.28(7) ibid.

(21) Or.59 R.61 (Edo) 2018; Or.55 R.61 (Delta) 2009 and Or.57 R.20 (Lagos) 2012, supra.

CHAPTER TWENTY-FOUR

COMPLETION OF ADMINISTRATION

In this book, the final process of completing the Administration of the estate of a deceased after obtaining Probate or Letters of Administration are grouped into the following:

i. Filing of Probate or Letters of Administration Account
ii. Filing of Vesting Assent

FILING OF PROBATE OR LETTERS OF ADMINISTRATION ACCOUNT

Upon the collection of grant by Executors or Administrators, Probate or Letters of Administration account forms, comprising form for Administration account and affidavit to be sworn to by persons concerned with the Administration of the deceased's estate are given together with the grant.

Thus:

"Every person to whom a grant of probate or letters of administration shall have been made and every administrator appointed by the Court shall, if called upon by the Court to do so, file in the Court the account of his administration, and shall thereafter file such further periodic accounts as the Court may direct until the completion of the administration".[(1)]

The first Administration account is filed after six months of the grant being issued, that is when the Executors or Administrators must have started administering the deceased's estate. Thereafter, periodic account is filed until the estate account shows a nil return. The accounts include inventory and payment vouchers in the hands of the Executors or Administrators relating thereto, receipts in support of any expenditure made in the estate, an affidavit in verification, etc.(2)

It is the duty of the Registrar to bring to the notice of the Court, the fact that any Executor or Administrator has failed to file his accounts as required by law.(3) The Court may on the application of any party interested or of its own motion, summon any Executor or Administrator who fails to file his accounts to show cause why he should not be punished. For a good cause shown, the Court may extend the time for such filing of accounts.(4) However, any Executor or Administrator who fails within any such period or extended time to file his accounts, is liable to a fine as the Court may deem fit to impose or imprisonment for a term not exceeding six months.(5)

Every accounts filed are open for inspection to all persons satisfying the Registrar as persons interested in the Administration of the deceased's estate.(6) It is pertinent to note that, if upon scrutiny, any Administration Account filed appears by reason of improper un-vouchered or unjustifiable entries or otherwise, such account is not a full and proper account, the person filing the account is given written notice to remedy such defects within a stipulated time reasonable for the purpose and on failure to remedy the defects within that stipulated time, the person who filed such defective account is deemed to have failed to file an account as required by Law and proceedings may be taken against such person accordingly.(7)

Where only personal property such as money in bank, pension and gratuity, fund with pension managers, shares etc is the administered estate, once the Administration Account filed has been considered and approved by the Registrar, the estate matter will then be regarded as closed and the Executors or

Administrators will be discharged and Certificate of Discharge will be issued.

FILING OF VESTING ASSENT

After obtaining Probate or Letters of Administration, Executors or Administrators are empowered to vest property right on individual beneficiaries.

Therefore:

> *"A personal representative may assent to the vesting in any person who (whether by devise, bequest, devolution, appropriation or otherwise) may be entitled thereto, either beneficially or as trustee or personal representative, of any estate or interest in real estate to which the testator or intestate was entitled or over which he exercised a general power of appointment by his Will, and which devolved upon the personal representative".*[(8)]

In line with the above law, Vesting means conferring ownership of property upon a person or investing a person with the full title to property while Assent can be reasonably interpreted as willingness. Vesting Assent therefore, is like a Court Order passing Legal Title in lieu of a Legal Conveyance.

REQUIREMENTS FOR A VALID ASSENT

An Assent to the vesting of a legal estate must be in writing, signed by the personal representative, that is, the Executors or Administrators, and must name the person or beneficiary in whose favour it is given and must also operate to vest in that beneficiary the legal estate or interest to which it relate and unless a contrary intention appears, the assent must relate back to the death of the deceased.[(9)] Therefore, any assent not in writing or in favour of a named person cannot be effectual to pass a legal estate or title.

Assent given in favour of individual beneficiaries are expected to be filed at the Registry.

Thus:

> *"Any person in whose favour an assent or conveyance of a legal estate is made by a personal representative may require that notice of the assent or conveyance be written or indorsed on or permanently annexed to the probate or letters of administration at the cost of the estate of the deceased, and that the probate or letters of administration be produced, at the like cost, to prove that the notice has been placed thereon or annexed thereto."*[(10)]

It is important to note that vesting assent relating to registered properties, equally required filing at the Lands Registry where such properties are registered. Also the Statutory Covenants implied by a person being expressed to convey as a Personal Representative may be implied in an Assent in like manner as in a conveyance by deed. However, no stamp duty is impose in respect of an Assent.[(11)]

By the Operation of Law, the real estate of a deceased Testator vest in the beneficiary of the estate when the personal representative of the deceased assent in writing to the vesting of the estate in the beneficiary. In other words, the real estate of deceased vests in the beneficiary only when a vesting assent is made by an Executor in relation to the estate. Thus a beneficiary cannot claim his share in the estate of the deceased Testator until the Executors have given their assent to the vesting of the property in him.[(12)]

Therefore a beneficiary cannot sue for any property devised to him or her under the Will when the said property is still vested in the Executor of the Will. Before a beneficiary can sue on a Will, there must be a vesting assent from the Executors or the beneficiary will join the Executors as co-plaintiffs in the suit. In the absence of any Vesting Assent, the beneficiary have no *Locus Standi* to sue unless the Executors are dead.(13)

Where both personal and real properties or where real property is solely the estate administered, after the vesting of property right on individual beneficiaries by the Executors or Administrators of the estate of the deceased and the estate account shows a nil return, the Executors or Administrators can then be discharge of their duties and the Executors or Administrators will be issued Certificate of Discharge, upon filing vesting assent.

Consequently, upon filing Administration Account which is deemed to be full and proper and vesting assent, the Executors or Administrators who had nothing more to administer in respect of a deceased's estate, are said to be discharged of their duties once they are issued Certificate of Discharge by the Registrar.(14) This means the completion of administration of such deceased's estate and the estate matter will be regarded as closed and the Administrators are also discharged from the Bond they entered into.

REFERENCES

(1) Or.58 R.41(1) (Edo) 2018; Or.54 R.41(1) (Delta) 2009 and Or.57 R.16(1) (Lagos) 2012,supra.

(2) Or.58 R.41(9) ibid; Or.54 R.41(9) ibid and Or.57 R.16(9) ibid. NOTE: It is essential that figures or amount must be substantiated by documents to be attached.

(3) Or.58 R.41(7) ibid; Or.54 R.41(7) ibid and Or.57 R.16(4) ibid.

(4) Or.58 R.41(4)(5) ibid; Or.54 R.41(4)(5) ibid (Delta) 2009 and Or.57 R.16(5)(6) ibid.

(5) Or.58 R.41(2)(6) ibid; Or.54 R41(2)(6) (Delta) 2009 and Or.57 R.16(2)(7) ibid.

(6) Or.58 R.41(8) ibid; Or.54 R.41(8) ibid and Or.57 R.16(3) ibid.

(7) Or.41(3) ibid; Or.54 R.41(3) ibid and Or.57 R.16(3) ibid.

(8) Section 40(1) AEL (Bendel) 1976, supra.

(9) Section 40(4)(2) ibid.

(10) Section 40(5) ibid.

(11) Section 40(3)(11) ibid.

(12) See the case of Unoka V. Agili (2007) 11 NWRL (pt,1044) p. 122.

(13) See Unoka V. Agili (2007) ibid.

(14) See Appendix 20 for specimen of Certificate of Discharge.

CHAPTER TWENTY- FIVE

INSTITUTING PROBATE COURT ACTION

All Probate Court Action arising from the State is commenced at the Main Registry of the Edo State High Court at Benin City. The Chief Judge has power to request the Court of any Judicial Division in the State to take measures, including the preservation of the property of the deceased within such Judicial Division.(1)

Thus:

> *"The Court shall when the circumstances of the case appear to require Forthwith on the death of a person, or as soon after, appoint and authorize an officer of the court, or some other fit person, to take possession of his property within its jurisdiction, or put it under seal and so keep it until it can be dealt with according to law."*(2)

It is of importance to note that, the estate of a deceased who died intestate is vested on the Chief Judge from the date of his death until grant of administration.(3)

THE NATURE OF PROCEEDINGS IN PROBATE COURT ACTION

In Probate Court Actions, the general nature of Court proceedings is as follows:

i. Probate matters take the same process as those obtain in civil claims.

   Thus:

   > *"Suits respecting probate or administration shall be instituted and carried on as nearly as may be in the like manner and subject to the same rules of*

procedure as suits in respect of ordinary claims."[4]

ii. The capacity in which a person brings Probate action must be stated.

Therefore:

> *"In probate actions, the originating process shall state whether the claimant claims as creditor, executor, administrator, beneficiary, next-of-kin or in any other capacity."*[5]

iii. The party must state with regard to every defense which is pleaded, what is the substance of the case on which it is intended to rely and where it is pleaded that the Testator was not of sound mind, memory and understanding, particulars of any specific instances of delusion must be delivered before the case is set down for trial and except by the leave of court, no evidence will be given of any other instances at the trial.[6]

iv. Where the claimant disputes the interest of the defendant, he must allege in his statements of claim that he denies the defendant's interest.[7]

v. The party opposing a Will may with his defense, give notice to the party setting up the Will that he merely insists upon the Will being proved in solemn form of Law and only intends to cross examine the witnesses produced in support of the Will and he shall thereupon be at liberty to do so and will not in any event be liable to pay the cost of the other side unless the Court finds that there was no reasonable ground for opposing the Will.[8]

It is pertinent to note that the following persons, namely:

i. The Executors or Administrators of a deceased person;
ii. The Trustees under any deed or instrument;
iii. A Person claiming to be interested in the relief sought as creditor, beneficiary, next-of-kin, trustee of a deceased person, etc

May takeout an originating summons for such relief as listed hereunder as may be specified by the summons and as the circumstances of the case may require, in respect of any of the following questions or matters:[9]

(a) Any question affecting the rights or interests of the person claiming to be creditor, beneficiary, next-of-kin, or trustee;
(b) The ascertainment of any class of creditors, beneficiary, next-of-kin or others;
(c) The furnishing of any particular accounts by the Executors, Administrators or Trustees and the vouching, when necessary of such account;
It is of importance to note that every judgment or order for a general account of the personal estate of a Testator or Intestatus, must contain a direction for any inquiry as to what parts of such personal estate are outstanding or indisposed of, unless the Court shall otherwise direct.[10]
(d) The payment into Court of any money in the hand of the Executors, Administrators or Trustees;
(e) Directing the Executors, Administrators or Trustees to do or abstain from doing any particular act, as Executors, Administrators or Trustees;

(f) The approval of any sale, purchase, compromise or other transaction;
(g) The determination of any question arising in the Administration of the estate or trust.

However, the issuing of summons under the above mentioned rule (order 59 Rule 88), does not interfere with any power vested in any Executor, Administrator or Trustee except so far as such interference may necessarily be involved in the particular relief sought.(11)

Also, the Executors, Administrators, Trustees, Credit, Beneficiary, Next-of-Kin, etc, may likewise apply and obtain an order for:

i. The Administration of the personal or real estate of the deceased;
ii. The Administration of the trust;
iii. Any act to be done or step to be taken, which the Court could have ordered to be done or taken if any such Administration Order as aforesaid, had previously been made.(12)

Upon an application for Administration or Execution of trust by a creditor or beneficiary under a Will, intestacy or deed of trust where no accounts or insufficient accounts have been rendered, the Court may, in addition to the powers already existing:

(a) Order that the application be stand over for a certain time, and that the Executors, Administrators or Trustees in the meantime, render to the Applicant, proper statement of their accounts, with an intimation that if this is not done, they will be made to pay the cost of the proceedings;

(b) When necessary, to prevent proceedings by other creditors or persons beneficially interested, make the usual Judgment or Order for Administration with a Proviso that no proceedings are to be taken under such Judgment or Order without the leave of Court.(13)

In Probate Court Action, after the Judgment or Order, as the case may be, the party who is victorious can then commence or continue with the application for grant of Probate or Letters of Administration and Certified True Copy of the Judgment or Order is produced and filed in the Registry. However, the Court is not bound to order Administration.

Thus:

> ***"it shall not be obligatory on the judge to pronounce or make judgment or order, whether on summons or otherwise, for the administration of any trust or of the estate of any deceased person if the questions between the parties can be properly determined without such judgment or order".**(14)*

SERVICE OF PROCESS IN PROBATE COURT ACTION AND PERSONS TO BE SERVED

Unless the Registrar or Probate rules otherwise direct, any notice or other document required to be given or served on any person may be served by leaving it at or by sending it by prepaid registered post to that person's address for service and if there is no address for service, his last known address.(15)

Where by the provision of Probate rules or any direction given by a Judge or Registrar, a notice of Motion or Summons required to be served on any person, it must be served not less than five days before the hearing of the Motion or

Summons.[16] By Leave of Court, service of a Writ of Summons may be allowed outside Nigeria.[17]

Persons to be served with summons relating to Probate Court Action include the following: [18]

(a) Where the Summons is taken out by an Executor, Administrator or Trustee, persons to be served are:

- (i) The persons whose rights or interest are sought to be affected;
- (ii) Any member or alleged member of class of creditors, beneficiary, next-of-kin or others (Regarding the issue of ascertainment of any class of creditors, beneficiary, etc under Order 59 Rule 88(b));
- (iii) Any person interested in taking accounts (Regarding the issue of furnishing account under Order 59 Rule 88(c));
- (iv) Any person interested in taking money (Relating to the issue of payment into Court, under Order 59 Rule 88(d));
- (v) The residuary legatees, nest-of-kin or the residuary devisees (with regard to the administration of trust under Order 59 Rule 89 (b));
- (vi) Any Executor, Administrator or Trustee who do not concur in the taking out of Summons.

(b) Where the Summons is taken out by any person other than the Executors, Administrators or Trustees, the Executors, Administrators or Trustees must be served.

It is important to note that a notice of Motion or Summons for the service of which no provision is made in the Probate rules must be served on such person or persons as the Judge or Registrar may direct.[(19)]

Also any person aggrieved by the decision or requirement of the Registrar may appeal by Summons to a Judge. And in the case of such appeal, if any person besides the appellant appeared or was represented before the Registrar from whose decision or requirement the appeal is brought, the Summons will be issued within seven (7) days for hearing on the first available day and must be served on every such person concerned.[(20)]

REFERENCES

(1) Or.58 R.1(2) & Or.59 R.6(2) (Edo) 2018 and Or.54 R.1(2) & Or.55 R.6(2) (Delta) 2009.

(2) Or.58 R.2 (Edo) 2018;Or.54 R.2 (Delta) 2009 and Or.57 R.2(1) (Lagos) 2012, supra.

(3) Section 10 AEL (Bendel) 1976, supra.

(4) Or.59 R.27,R.79 & Or.58 R.15 (Edo) 2018; Or.55 R.27,R.79 & Or.54 R.15 (Delta) 2009 and Or.60 R.1 (Lagos) 2012,supra.

(5) Or.59 R81 (Edo) 2018; Or.55 R.81 (Delta) 2009 and Or.60 R.2 supra.

(6) Or.59 R.83 (Edo) 2018; Or.55 R.83 (Delta) 2009 and Or.60 R.4 supra.

(7) Or.59 R.84 (Edo) 2018; Or.55 R.84 (Delta) 2009 and Or.60 R.5 supra.

(8) Or.59 R.85 (Edo) 2018; Or.55 R.85 (Delta) 2009 and Or.60 R.6 ,supra.

(9) Or.59 R.88 (Edo) 2018; Or.55 R.88 (Delta),2009 and Or.60 R.9 supra.

(10) Or.59 R.86 (Edo) 2018; Or.55 R.86 (Delta) 2009, and Or.60 R.7 supra

(11) Or.59 R. 93 (Edo) 2018; Or.55 R.93 (Delta) 2009, and Or.6o R.12 supra.

(12) Or.59 R.89 (Edo) 2018; Or.55 R.89 (Delta) 2009, and Or.60 R.10 supra.

(13) Or.59 R.92 (Edo) 2018; Or.55 R.92 (Delta) 2009, and Or.60 R.14 supra.

(14) Or.59 R.91 (Edo) 2018; Or,55 R.91 (Delta) 2009, and Or.60 R.13 supra.

(15) Or.59 R.75 (Edo) 2018; Or.55 R.75 (Delta) 2009, and Or.60 R.21 supra.

(16) Or.59 R.74(2) (Edo) 2018; Or.55 R.74(2) (Delta) 2009, and Or.60 R.20(2) supra.

(17) Or.59 R.82 (Edo) 2018; Or.55 R.82 (Delta), and Or.60 R.3 supra.

(18) Or.59 R.90 (Edo) 2018; Or.55 R.90 (Delta) 2009, and Or.60 R.11 supra.

(19) Or.59 R.74(1) (Edo) 2018; Or.55 R.74(1) (Delta) 2009, and Or.60 R.20(1) supra.

(20) Or.59 R.73 (Edo) 2018 and Or.55 R.73 (Delta) 2009, supra.

APPENDICES

IN THE HIGH OF JUSTICE
EDO STATE OF NIGERIA
ADMINISTRATION BOND (WITHOUT WILL)

IN THE MATTER OF ___________________DECEASED

KNOWN ALL MEN BY THESE PRESENT, that we, ____ ____ ______________________________________ are jointly and severally bound unto ______________________ the Probate Registrar of the High Court of Justice, Edo State of Nigeria, in the sum of ________ Naira, to be paid to the said _________ of the Probate Registrar of the said Court for the Time being; for which payment we bind ourselves and each of us, for himself, in the whole, our and each of our heirs, executors, and administrators, firmly by these presents. Sealed with our seals, Dated the _________ day of _______________, 20________.

The condition of the above written obligation is such, that if the above-named_______________, the intended Administrator of the real and personal property of __________________ late of __________________ deceased, who died on the __________ day _________________, 20 _____ do make a true perfect inventory of the real And personal property of the deceased which has or shall come into ____________ possession, or into possession of any person for ________________ and the sum so made exhibit into the High Court of Justice, Edo State of Nigeria as required by law so do; and the same real and personal property and all other real and Personal property of the deceased, which shall at any time after the making an exhibition of such inventory come into the possession of the said ___________________ Or any person for _______________ do, we and truly administer according to law (that is to say) ; do pay the debts which the deceased owed at ________________ death, and all the residue the said real and personal property; do deliver and pay to such person as shall be entitled hereto, by law, and further do make a true and just account of _____________ administration as lawfully require; and in case it shall hereafter appear that any Will was made by the deceased, and the executor, or executors, or other persons therein named, do exhibit the same for probate, then if the said ___________________being thereunto required, do duly render and deliver us the Letters of Administration granted to___________ then this obligation shall be void, otherwise shall remain in full Force.

Signed, sealed and delivered by the above-named.) L.S

) L.S

In the presence of) L.S

) L.S

COMMISSIONER FOR OATHS.

IN THE HIGH COURT OF JUSTICE
EDO STATE OF NIGERIA
IN THE BENIN JUDICIAL DIVISION

AFFIDAVIT TO ADMINISTER PART OF THE ESTATE OF
____________________ DECEASED

I, ________________________ (Female) Christian, Citizen of the Federal Republic of Nigeria, residing at No. ________________ do hereby depose on Oath and state as follows:

That I am the declarant herein in the matter of my late father

____

1. That I have the consent of the second applicant to depose to this affidavit.
2. That my late father estate comprises real and personal property, but due to the difficulty and delay in ascertaining the exact location of the real property, I intend to administer only the personal property for now.
3. That by this affidavit, I hereby suspend the Administration of the real property.
4. That the Probate Registrar should please take note.
5. AND that I swear to this affidavit in good faith, believing the contents to be true and correct in accordance with the Statutory Declaration Oath Laws of 1976, also applicable in Edo State.

....
DECLARANT

SWORN TO AT THE COURT
REGISTRY, BENIN CITY,
THIS .... DAY OF .... 20..........
BEFORE ME

COMMISSIONER FOR OATHS

IN THE HIGH COURT OF JUSTICE
EDO STATE OF NIGERIA
IN THE BENJN JUDICIAL DIVISION

AFFIDAVIT FOR FURTHER SECURITY

I, ____________________ (Female), a Christian, Citizen of the Federal Republic of Nigeria, residing at No. ______________, do hereby depose on Oath and state as follows:

1. That I am the declarant herein and the second Administrator in the estate of my mother, late ____________________
2. That I have the consent of the first Administrator, ______________________ to depose to this affidavit.
3. That Letters of Administration was earlier granted to us on the _____ day of _____, 20______, and the estate covered by the Letters of Administration was Money in Bank only.
4. That we discovered the deceased had some Arrears of Pension and gratuity after the Letters of Administration was granted, hence the need for this affidavit
5. That we pray the Probate Registrar to please grant us Certificate of Further Security to enable us claim the Arrears of Pension and Gratuity
6. AND that I swear to this affidavit in good faith, believing the contents to be true and correct in accordance with the Statutory Declaration Oath Laws of 1976, also applicable in Edo State.

....

DECLARANT

SWORN TO AT THE PROBATE REGISTRY, BENIN CITY,

THIS .... DAY OF ...., 20.............

BEFORE ME

COMMISSIONER FOR OATHS

IN THE HIGH OF JUSTICE
EDO STATE OF NIGERIA
IN THE BENIN JUDICIAL DIVISION

AFFIDAVIT FOR ADDITIONAL PERSONAL REPRESENTATIVE/JOINDER OF ADMINISTRATOR

I, ___________________ (Male) Christian, Citizen of the Federal Republic of Nigeria, residing at No.____________________, do hereby depose on Oath and state as follows:

1. That I am the declarant herein in the matter of my late father ____________________
2. That I have the consent of the second applicant to depose to this affidavit.
3. That there arose a need for ______________ to co-administer our late father's estate as the third Applicant/Administrator.
4. That the Probate Registrar should please take note.
5. AND that I swear to this affidavit in good faith, believing the contents to be true and correct in accordance with the Statutory Declaration Oath Laws of 1976, also applicable in Edo State.

....
DECLARANT

SWORN TO AT THE HIGH COURT
REGISTRY, BENIN CITY,
THIS .... DAY OF .... 20...........

BEFORE ME

COMMISSIONER FOR OATHS

IN THE HIGH COURT OF JUSTICE
EDO STATE OF NIGERIA
IN THE BENIN JUDICIAL DIVISION

AFFIDAVIT OF DEATH

I, ______________________ (Male), Christian, Citizen of the Federal Republic of Nigeria, residing at No, _______________. Do hereby depose on Oath and state as follows:

1. That I am the declarant herein
2. That late _____________________________ was my father.
3. That late __________________________ died on the ____day of __________ 20_____ at the age of __________ years.
4. That the said late __________________________ died after a brief illness in _____________
5. That this affidavit is needed to enable me obtain his Death Certificate from the National Population Commission for record purpose
6. That I depose to this affidavit for record purpose and To Whom It May Concern should please take note
7. AND that I swear to this affidavit in good faith, believing the contents to be true and correct in accordance with the Statutory Declaration Oath Laws of 1976, also applicable in Edo State

....
DECLARANT

SWORN TO AT THE HIGH
REGISTRY, BENIN CITY,
DATED THIS .... DAY OF ...., 20...........

BEFORE ME

COMMISSIONER FOR OATHS

IN THE HIGH COURT OF JUSTICE
EDO STATE OF NIGERIA
(PROBATE REGISTRY)

AFFIDAVIT OF ATTESTING WITNESS OF WILL

IN the matter of .... Deceased

I, ... of ....

make Oath and say:

1. That I am one of the subscribing witness to the last WILL of ....late of .... Deceased (the said Will being now hereto annexed), bearing date the ...... day of ...., 20 .... and that the Testat .... executed the said WILL on the day of the date thereof by .... the other subscribed witness thereto .... of us being present at the same time, and we thereupon attested and subscribed the said WILL in the presence of the Testat..
2. That the said WILL was, previously to the execution thereof as aforesaid correctly interpreted to the Testat .... in our presence by .... Of .... and the Testat .... appeared perfectly to understand the same.

....
Declarant

Sworn to at .... this .... Day of ...., 20......

BEFORE ME,

....

COMMISSIONER FOR OATHS

IN THE HIGH OF JUSTICE
EDO STATE OF NIGERIA

FORM OF AFFIDAVIT TO BE SWORN BY PERSONS CONCERNED WITH THE ADMINISTRATION OF ESTATES

(VERIFICATION OF AN ADMINISTRATION ACCOUNT)

In the matter of the Administration of the estate of the late………………… ………………………………..: Deceased

I, ………………………………..make oath and say as follows:

1. I was by order of the Court dated ……. day of ……………, 20 …. appointed one of the Administrators of the estate of ……………………………… who died at …………….. on the …… day of …………., 20 ……
2. I attach hereto a cash account marked Exhibit " " showing accurately the assets of the deceased received by us (the administrators) and payments made by us in respect of liabilities due from the estate, supported by relevant receipts marked Exhibit " " " " respectively.
3. To the best of my information, knowledge and belief there are no other assets of the deceased nor are there any outstanding liabilities.

…………….
Administrator

SWORN at ……… this ….. day of ……… 20 …..

BEFORE ME

COMMISSIONER FOR OATHS

IN THE HIGH OF JUSTICE
EDO STATE OF NIGERIA
IN THE BENIN JUDICIAL DIVISION

AFFIDAVIT OF ATTESTATION

I, ________________ (Male), a Christian, Citizen of the Federal Republic of Nigeria, residing at No. ____________________, do hereby depose on Oath and state as follows:

1. That I am the declarant herein.
2. That I attest to the signatures on the reply (Consent Letter) to the Notice of Application served on my children:

   Mr. ______________________________

   Miss. ____________________________

   Mr. ______________________________
3. That the Probate Registrar should please take note.
4. AND that I swear to this affidavit in good faith, believing the contents to be true and correct in accordance with the Statutory Declaration Oath Laws of 1976, also applicable in Edo State.

....

DECLARANT

SWORN TO AT THE HIGH COURT
REGISTRY, BENIN CITY,
THIS .... DAY OF .... , 20.........

BEFORE ME

COMMISSIONER FOR OATHS

IN THE HIGH OF JUSTICE
EDO STATE OF NIGERIA
IN THE BENIN JUDICIAL DIVISION
AFFIDAVIT OF CONSENT

I, ______________ (Female), a Christian, Citizen of the Federal Republic of Nigeria, residing at No. ________________, do hereby depose on Oath state as follows:

1. That I am the declarant herein
2. That this affidavit is sworn in respect of the estate of my mother late______________________
3. That Letters of Administration (Without Will) dated _____ day of _______ was earlier granted to my brothers, ______________________ and _____________ in respect of the above-named deceased's estate
4. That I am aware that ______________, who is the second Administrator is presently residing outside the country
5. That this has made the Administration of the said estate unsustainable and there arose a need to substitute _________
6. That I have agreed to co-administer the said estate with my elder brother, the first Administrator, _________________
7. That the Probate Registrar should please take note
8. AND that I swear to this affidavit in good faith, believing the contents to be true and correct in accordance with the Statutory Declaration Oath Laws of 1976, also applicable in Edo State.

....
DECLARANT

SWORN TO AT THE HIGH COURT
REGISTRY, BENIN CITY,
DATED THIS ...... DAY OF .... 20 ......

BEFORE ME
COMMISSIONER FOR OATHS

IN THE HIGH OF JUSTICE
EDO STATE OF NIGERIA
IN THE BENIN JUDICIAL DIVISION

AFFIDAVIT OF IDENTITY/ADDITIONAL NAME

I, ______________________ (Male), a Christian, Citizen of the Federal Republic of Nigeria, residing at No. _______________, do hereby depose on Oath and state as follows:

1. That I am the declarant herein
2. That late ______________________________ was my father
3. That while alive he was known, called and addressed as ____________________
4. That when his Death Certificate was issued ____________ was used. While ______________ was omitted, hence the need for this affidavit
5. That the purpose of this affidavit is to reconcile his name to reflect ___________
6. That the Probate Registrar and **TO WHOM IT MAY CONCERN** should please take note.
7. AND that I swear to this affidavit in good faith, believing the contents to be true and correct in accordance with the Statutory Declaration Oath Laws of 1976, also applicable in Edo State.

....
DECLARANT

SWORN TO AT THE HIGH COURT
REGISTRY, BENIN CITY,
DATED THIS ...... DAY OF .... 20...........

BEFORE ME

COMMISSIONER FOR OATHS

IN THE HIGH OF JUSTICE
EDO STATE OF NIGERIA
IN THE BENIN JUDICIAL DIVISION

AFFIDAVIT OF LOST OF ORIGINAL DEATH CERTIFICATE

I, ____________________ (Female), a Christian, Citizen of the Federal Republic of Nigeria, residing at No. _______________, do hereby depose on Oath and state as follows:

1. That I am the declarant herein
2. That late _________________ was my father
3. That the _________________ died on the ___ day of ______ at the age of ______ years
4. That the said _________________ died after a brief illness in the University of Benin Teaching Hospital, Benin City and a Death Certificate was duly issued to that effect.
5. That the said Death Certificate got missing in transit and all effort to recover same has proved abortive.
6. That the Probate Registrar and TO WHOM IT MAY CONCERN should please take note.
7. AND that I swear to this affidavit in good faith, believing the contents to be true and correct in accordance with the Statutory Declaration Oath Laws of 1976, also applicable in Edo State.

....
DECLARANT

SWORN TO AT THE HIGH COURT
REGISTRY, BENIN CITY,
DATED THIS ...... DAY OF .... 20..........

BEFORE ME

COMMISSIONER FOR OATHS

IN THE HIGH OF JUSTICE
EDO STATE OF NIGERIA
IN THE BENIN JUDICIAL DIVISION

AFFIDAVIT OF SUBSTITUTION

I, ________________ (Male), a Christian, Citizen of the Federal Republic of Nigeria, residing at No. ______________ do hereby depose on Oath and state as follows:

1. That I am the declarant herein
2. That this affidavit is sworn in respect of the estate of my late mother, _________
3. That Letters of Administration dated ____ day of _______, 20 ______ was earlier granted to us, ______ and _______, sons of the deceased in respect of the above named estate.
4. That I am the first Administrator of the said estate
5. That the second Administrator, ______________ travelled outside the country on the ___ day of _____, 20 ____.
6. That I now wish to substitute the second Administrator with my young brother, _______________, for effective Administration of the said estate
7. That the Probate Registrar should please take note
8. AND that I swear to this affidavit in good faith, believing the contents to be true and correct in accordance with the Statutory Declaration Oath Laws of 1976, also applicable in Edo State.

....
DECLARANT

SWORN TO AT HIGH COURT
REGISTRY, BENIN CITY,
DATED THIS _____ DAY OF _________, 20_____

BEFORE ME

COMMISSIONER FOR OATHS

IN THE HIGH OF JUSTICE
EDO STATE OF NIGERIA
IN THE BENIN JUDICIAL DIVISION

AFFIDAVIT OF WITNESS

I, ______________________ (male), a Christian, Citizen of the Federal Republic of Nigeria, residing at No, _______________, do hereby depose on Oath and state as follows:

1. That I am the declarant herein
2. That I witnessed the signing of the reply to the Notice of Application served on my brothers:
   Mr. ________________________________
   Mr. ________________________________
   Mr. ________________________________
3. That the Probate Registrar should please take note
4. AND that I swear to this affidavit in good faith, believing the contents to be true and correct in accordance with the Statutory Declaration Oath Laws of 1976, also applicable in Edo State.

....
DECLARANT

SWORN TO AT THE HIGH COURT REGISTRY, BENIN CITY,
DATED THIS .... DAY OF ...., 20............

BEFORE ME

COMMISSIONER FOR OATHS

FORM 55

(O. 59, R. 57 (9) & 58 (6))
Appearance to Warning or Citation

IN THE HIGH COURT OF EDO STATE
PROBATE REGISTRY

Suit No............

Caveat No.......... dated the .... day of ...... 20 ....
Citation dated the ...... day of .... 20 ....

Full name and address of the deceased: ....
Full name and address of person warning (Citor): ....
Interest of person warning (or Citor): ....
Full name and address of Caveator (or person cited): ....
Date of Will ....
Interest of Caveator: ....
Enter an appearance for the above-named Caveator (or person cited) ....
In this matter ....

DATED this ..... Day of ...., 20..............

Whose address, for service is ....

(Signed) ....

....
.Legal Practitioner.
(or "in person")

IN THE HIGH COURT OF JUSTICE
EDO STATE OF NIGERIA

APPLICATION FOR PROBATE OR LETTERS OF ADMINISTRATION

IN THE Matter of the Estate of ……………………. Deceased
I/We……………………………………………………..…
of …..……………………………………………………
hereby make application for Probate/Letters of Administration (Will Annexed) to administer the estate of ………………., late of ………………… who died on the …. day of ……, 20 …. at ……………………………

2. The deceased was my ……………………………….
3. The deceased left real property to the value of N ……………………………….. All/part of which is situated within the jurisdiction of the High Court of the Edo State.
4. The deceased left personal property to the value of N……………….All/part……………………………………
5. The inventory attached hereto contains particulars of the personal property of the deceased died possessed and in the respect of which a grant is required.
6. Particulars of Real estate left by the deceased and in the respect of which a grant is required are also attached.

……………………………………….
…………………………………..
……………………………………
…………………………………..
……………………………………
Date………………………………

IN THE HIGH COURT OF JUSTICE
EDO STATE OF NIGERIA
(PROBATE REGISTRY)

APPLICATION FOR SURETYSHIP

IN THE MATTER OF THE ESTATE OF……… DECEASED

(1) Name of Surety ……………………………………………

(2) Address ……………………………………………………

(3) Occupation ……………………………………………….

(4) If employed, place of Employment ………………………

(5) Salary or Income per annum …………………………..

(6) Banking Account:

(a) Savings ……………………………………

(b) Current ……………………………………

(c) Fixed Deposit ………………………………

(7) Real Property

(a) Situation ……………………………………

(b) Value ……………………………………

(c) Mortgaged …………………………………

(8) Investments (give particulars) ……………………………

DATED this …… day of ………………20 ……………

………………

Signature

This surety has been examined by me and found suitable. He is recommended for approval.

…………………………….

Chief/Senior/Magistrate

APPROVED

……………………...

Probate Registrar

PED/………/…….
Probate Registry,
High Court of Justice,
Benin City.
Date: ________________

BANK CERTIFICATE

I hereby certify that ______________________ has/have applied for Letters of Administration of the real and personal property of ____, deceased and has/have authority to inquire on my behalf as to any sum standing to the credit of the deceased in the books of any book or as to any debts due to the deceased by any person.

PROBATE REGISTRAR

FORM 53

(O.59, R. 57 (2), (3)

CAVEAT

IN THE HIGH COURT OF EDO STATE

PROBATE REGISTRY

Suit No……………..

Let no grant be sealed in the estate of ………………., deceased who died on the ….. Day of ……. 20 …… at …………….. without notice to ………………………………………

DATED this ………… Day of ………. 20…………….
(Signed)…………………………………………………
Legal Practitioner for the said Caveator whose address for service is ……………………………………

EDO STATE JUDICIARY
OFFICE OF THE PROBATE REGISTRAR
(PROBATE REGISTRY)
HIGH COURT OF JUSTICE
BENIN CITY

PED/……./………..

CERTIFICATE FOR FURTHER SECURITY IN THE MATTER OF THE ESTATE OF ____________ DECEASED
I, ______________________, ESQ the probate Registrar of the High Court of Justice, Edo State of Nigeria, do hereby certify that the Gross Value of the Estate of ____________________________, originally estimated at ₦__________ (amount in words} only has been revalued at the sum of ₦______________ (amount in words) only and full security has been given for the increase over the original value.

Letters of Administration had earlier been granted on the day of ____, 20____ to ___ and _____, sons of the deceased.

DATED IN BENIN CITY, THIS …… DAY OF ……, 20 …

ESTATE SWORN TO:-

SHARES

______________________, **ESQ.**
PROBATE REGISTRAR

EDO STATE JUDICIARY
OFFICE OF THE PROBATE REGISTRAR
(PROBATE REGISTRY)
HIGH COURT OF JUSTICE

……… , 20…………

PED/………../…………
(1) MRS. ………………..
(2) CHIEF………………..
All of No. ____________________

____

CERTIFICATE OF DISCHARGE

RE: ______________________________________ DECEASED

I refer to the Administration Account filed on the__________ day of ____________, 20_______ in respect of the above-named deceased's estate and write to inform you that after careful consideration and approval of the said Administration Account, this estate matter is now regarded as closed and you are therefore discharged from the Bond you entered into on the ___ day of _________, 20____ for the sum of ₦________ (amount in words).

DATED AT BENIN CITY, THIS ___ DAY OF _____, 20 __

_____________________, **ESQ**
PROBATE REGISTRAR

EDO STATE JUDICIARY
OFFICE OF THE PROBATE REGISTRAR
(PROBATE REGISTRY)
HIGH COURT OF JUSTICE
BENIN CITY

CERTIFICATE OF SUBSTITUTION

PED/………/…………
YOUR REF:……………………

IN THE MATTER OF THE ESTATE
OF__________________________ DECEASED

WHEREAS Letters of Administration in respect of the estate of ________________________ Deceased, who died on the ____ day of ________, 20 ____ intestate was granted to ____________________ and ____________, widow and brother respectively of the deceased on the _____ day of ______, 20 ___

UPON the death of the second Administrator, ______________ on the ___ day of _______, 20____, there arose a need for his substitution with ____________________.

NOW, _______________________, son of the deceased hereby substitute the late Administrator, _________________ and he is authorized to co-administer the estate with _______________________ in the interest of the beneficiaries.

DATED IN BENIN CITY, THIS …… DAY OF……, 20 ……

_______________________, **ESQ**
PROBATE REGISTRAR

Seal of Court

IN THE HIGH COURT OF JUSTICE
EDO STATE OF NIGREIA
DECLARATION AS TO NEXT-OF -KIN

Name of the Deceased ___________________________________

Title(s) First Name Other Names(If any) Surname

Native Place of the Deceased: ___________________________

Village L.G.A. State

Name of Wife/Wives or Husband of the Deceased _________

____

Address of Wife/Wives or Husband of the Deceased { ________________ ________________ ________________

Form of Marriage i.e. Native Law & Custom or Marriage Act _______________

Year of Marriage ________________

Names and ages of children above 18 years	Mother of each child and address.
______________________	______________________
______________________	______________________
______________________	______________________
______________________	______________________

Names and ages of children below 18 years	Names & address of mother or who the minor lives with
______________________	______________________
______________________	______________________
______________________	______________________
______________________	______________________

Deceased Father's Name:__________ Names and address of Deceased relation(s):

____

Deceased Mother's Name: ___________________________

Address of Deceased parents: ___________________________

____

Names of Applicants;

I/We:

____

So solemnly and sincerely make the above Declaration conscientiously believing the same to be true and correct and by virtue of the Statutory Declaration Law of Bendel State, 1976 as applicable in Edo State.

Declared at:_____ Signature of Declarant (1) ____________________

(2) ____________________

(3) ____________________

(4) ____________________

This________ day of _________

BEFORE ME

____

COMMISSIONER FOR OATHS

If space provided is insufficient, particulars may be put on separate papers, strike out any paragraph not applicable.

IN THE HIGH COURT OF JUSTICE
EDO STATE OF NIGERIA

INVENTORY

In the name of .... Deceased
A true declaration of all the personal property of ....
Late of ...., deceased, who died on the .... day of ...., 20 ...., at ....
and had at the time of his/her death his/her fixed place of abode at.................................. within the jurisdiction of this Court, which has at any time since his/her death come to the Possession or knowledge of .... the Administrator/Administratrix with the Will Annexed of the said .... made and exhibited upon and by virtue of the Oath of the and .... as follows:

First We/I declare that the deceased was at the time of his /her death possessed of or entitled to---

			₦	K
1. Money in Bank:				
(a) Savings Bank	..	..	..	..
(b) Current Account	..	..	..	..
(c) Deposit Account	..	..	..	..
2. Money found at Home	..	..	..	..
3. Debts due to the Deceased	..	..	..	..
4. Particulars and value of property held by the deceased as Lessee		..	..	..
5. Stock in Trade		..	..	..
6. Motor vehicles (Buses, Motor Car, Motor Cycles)		..	..	..
7. Personal Chattels (in detail)		..	..	..
		Carried forward	..	..

	₦	K
Brought forward	..	..
Total	..	..

Lastly, We/I say that no personal property of the deceased has at any time since his/her death come to our/my possession or knowledge, save as in hereinbefore set forth.

The foregoing having been first read over and interpreted to the illiterate deponents:

....	....
....	1. ....
In the .... language	2. ....
By.........when............	3. ....
Seemed perfectly to understand	4. ....
same before affixing	
thumb prints thereon	

....

Signature of Declarants

On the .... day of ......, 20......

The said........................... }
.... } were/was duly
.... }

Sworn to the truth of the above written inventory.

Before Me

____

Commissioner for Oath

JUSTIFICATION OF SURETIES

IN THE HIGH COURT OF JUSTICE
EDO STATE OF NIGERIA

PROBATE REGISTRY

IN THE MATTER OF……………….………………. Deceased

We…………………………………………………………

of…………………………………………………………

and…………………………………………………………

of…………………………………………………………

Severally make Oath and say, that we are the proposed sureties in the penal sum of ……………………………………. naira on behalf of ………………………………………. the intended Administrator …………………………….. of the personal and real property of ………………………………. late of ……………………………………………… deceased, for his faithful administration thereof.

And I the said ..…………………………………………

for myself, make Oath and say, that I am, after payment of all my just debts, well and

Truly worth in money and effects the sum of ………………………………………… naira

And I the said …..………………………………………

for myself, make Oath and say, that I am , after payment of all my just debts, well and truly worth in money and effects the of ………………………………………………………………… naira

(1) Signature of Surety ………………………

(2) Signature of Surety ………………………

SWORN TO AT …… THIS …… DAY OF …………, 20 ……

Before Me

……………………………………..

Commissioner For Oaths

PED/…………/……………

IN THE HIGH COURT OF JUSTICE
EDO STATE OF NIGERIA

LETTERS OF ADMINISTRATION (WITHOUT WILL)

BE IT KNOWN that on the …… day of …………, 20 …. Letters of Administration of the real and personal property of ……………………………………………………………… late of ……………………………………………………………… Deceased, who died on the ……… Day of ……………, 20 ….. in …………………………Intestate, and who had at the time of death his/her fixed place of abode at ………………………… within the jurisdiction of this Court, were granted by the Court to ……………………… and ………………………….. of No……………………………………………………………, The Son and Daughter of the said Intestate, they having been first duly sworn.

MONEY IN BANK SHARES

REAL PROPERTIES

………………………, **ESQ**
PROBATE REGISTRAR

(Seal of Court)

SCHEDULE OF FEES

File and Tag	....	N
Application for Letters of Administration	....	N
Swearing persons to inventory	....	N
Filing inventory form	....	N
Swearing persons to Declaration as to Next-of- Kin form	..	N
Filing Declaration as to Next-of-Kin form	....	N
Legal Notice Publication	....	N
Oath in Oath for Administration form	....	N
Filing Oath for Administration form	....	N
Attestation signatures on Bond	....	N
Filing Administration Bond form	....	N
Drawing up of Administration Decree	....	N
Oath in and filing renunciation form	....	N
Oath in and filing Justification of Sureties form	......	N
Estate fees	......	N

RECEIPTS LISTED

PR/ CR NO.	of	.../...../2019	....	N
PR/ CR NO.	of	.../...../2019	....	N
PR/ CR NO.	of	.../...../2019	....	N
PR/CR NO.	of	.../...../2019	....	N

LETTER FORWARDING FIRST SET OF PROBATE FORMS

OUR REF; NO. PED/___ /____

Probate Registry,
High Court of Justice,
Benin City.
___/ ___ 20 ____

Sir / Madam,

ESTATE OF ______________________________ DECEASED

1. With reference to your letter dated ___________________ I forward herewith one Inventory and Declaration as to Next - of-Kin forms for completion, when completed they should be sworn to before a Commissioner for Oaths.
2. The following fees payable should be remitted to me :

(a) File and Tag	N
(b) Application for Letters of Administration	N
(c) Filing Inventory form of Administration	N
(d) Filing Declaration as to Next-of Kin form	N
(e) Printing & Publication of Legal Notice	N
	________________
	________________

3. Each Deponent will pay an additional fee of Four Hundred Naira to the Commissioner for Oaths for swearing to the truth of the Inventory and the Declaration as to Next-of-Kin forms. Estate fee will be determined when Inventory is filed.
4. The attached Bank Certificate should be produced to the Bank(s) operating in the place of abode of the deceased before his/her death, for endorsement as to the amount of money standing to the credit of the deceased at the date of

death. The Certificate together with the completed forms should be forwarded to this Registry.

5. Please furnish proof of death of the deceased by supplying the Original Death Certificate issued by the Medical Practitioner who treated the deceased prior to his/her death or a Certificate issued by the National Population Commission testifying to the date and place of death of the deceased.
6. The Certificate of Marriage between the spouses (if any) should be forwarded to the Probate Registrar.
7. The attached application form for Letters of Administration should be completed by you and your Co-applicant(s).

Yours Faithfully

For: PROBATE REGISTRAR

____

____

____

____

LETTER FORWARDING SECOND SET OF PROBATE FORMS

OUR REF; NO. PED /___/ ____
Probate Registry.
High Court of Justice,
Benin City.
____/ _____ 20 ____

SIR/MADAM,

ESTATE OF ______________________________ DECEASED

I forward herewith few copies of the Legal Notice Publication in the above matter together with three forms namely:-

(1) Justification of Sureties, (2) Oath for Administration and (3) Administration Bond , for completion and early return.

(2) The Bond which should be executed in the name of ____________________________ Probate Registrar, Edo State of Nigeria, Benin City should be in the Penal Sum of N___________

(3) Your Sureties should be presented before the _________________________ for examination as to their means. They will be required to produce evidence of their fitness to stand surety in the amount in paragraph 2.

(4) The following fees payable should be remitted to this office

(A)	Filing Oath for Administration	...	N
(B)	Filing Justification Sureties	...	N
(C)	Filing Administration Bond	...	N
(D)	Drawing up Administration Decree	...	N
(E)	Estate Fee	... ...	N

____

____

(5) The forms must be sworn before ____________________ ________ to whom the sum of N ______________ being swearing and attestation fees on the forms are payable.

Yours Faithfully,

For: PROBATE REGISTRAR

____

____

____

____

OUR REF: NO. PED/…./…/ ….

Probate Registrar
High Court of Justice
Benin City.

…......., 20……

The Chief Magistrate,
Magistrate's Court
………………………………

I am directed to refer overleaf for your information, please.

2. You should please return to this office the attached Suretyship forms duly completed if you are Satisfied as to the suitability of the Sureties. It will also be necessary for you to inspect the real property and Bank Account Savings Books, if these are declared in the Suretyship forms.

For: PROBATE REGISTRAR

LETTER FORWARDING FORMS FOR PROBATE

OUR REF NO. PED/___/_____
Probate Registrar,
High Court of Justice,
Benin City.
_____/_________ 20_______

SIR/MADAM,

ESTATE OF _______________________ DECEASED

With reference to your letter of ______________________

I forward herewith Affidavit of Witness of Will, Oath for Executor and Inventory forms for completion and return.

2. The attached Bank Certificate should be produced to the Banks operating in the place of abode of the deceased before his /her death, for endorsement as to the amount of money standing to the credit of the deceased at the date of death. Any amount so endorsed should be included in the Inventory form. The Bank Certificate together with the completed forms should be forwarded to this Registry.
3. The following fees which are payable should be remitted to this office.

	N	K
Application for Probate … …		
Filing Will … …		
Filing Oath for Executor … …		
Filing Inventory form … …		
Filing of Affidavit of Witness of Will … …		
Sealing Copy of Will … …		
Marking …… Exhibit at……..each … …		
Copying and Certifying ………. folios of Will at ……….. per folio … …		

____

____

Estate fee will be determined when Inventory form is filed.

4. A fee of N........... be paid by each deponent as swearing fee on Affidavit of Witness of Will, Oath for executor and Inventory to the Commissioner for Oaths who will administer the Oath.
5. Please furnish proof of death of the deceased by supplying the Original Death Certificate issued by the Medical Practitioner who treated the deceased prior to his/her death or a Certificate issued by the Local Government Council of the area where the deceased died testifying to the date and place of death of the deceased.
6. The attached Application form for Probate should be completed by you and your Co-executors (if any).

Yours Faithfully

For—PROBATE REGISTRAR

____

____

EDO STATE JUDICIARY
OFFICE OF THE PROBATE REGISTRAR
(PROBATE REGISTRY)
HIGH COURT OF JUSTICE
BENIN CITY

LETTER CALLING FOR FIGURES

OUR REF: PED/……./……../ …….., 20……
YOUR REF:…………………

The Manager
Benefit Department,
……………………
……………………

ESTATE OF ……………………………. DECEASED

I am directed to inform you that Mrs. …………………… and Mr.…………………………., Widow and Son respectively of the above-named deceased have applied to this office for a grant of Letters of Administration in respect of the deceased's estate. The deceased was until his death on the …. day of ……., 20 .., a retired staff of ……………………………………..

It will be appreciated if you furnish this office with the figures representing the gratuity and pension for five years due to the deceased's estate to enable the applicants declare same on the Inventory form filed here by them.

Your early action will be appreciated, please.

…………………………...
For: PROBATE REGISTRAR

EDO STATE JUDICIARY
OFFICE OF THE PROBATE REGISTRAR
(PROBATE REGISTRY)
HIGH COURT OF JUSTICE
BENIN CITY

LETTER FOR FINANCIAL ASSISTANCE

YOUR REF………………
OUR REF: PED/……./…… ….., 20…

The Manager,
………………..Bank Plc.,
……………… Branch,
Benin City.

ESTATE OF ______________________ DECEASED

Mr……………………….., died on the … day of ………, 20…… testate/intestate. Consequently, MR …………………… and Miss……………………., son and daughter respectively of the deceased have applied for a grant of Letters of Administration. The application is being processed, but before the grant can be made, they are expected to pay an Estate fee chargeable on the value of the estate of the deceased.

An Inventory of the property of the deceased filed in this office by the applicants shows that the deceased had a balance of N……………………………(amount in words) only in his account with your Bank. The applicants have applied for Financial Assistance to enable them pay the Estate fee. Attached is a copy of their application to the Probate Registrar seeking Financial Assistance by way of releasing the sum of N…………………… (amount in words) only to meet with the above demand.

The application having been approved by this office, you are therefore requested to release the sum of N.................. (amount in words) only from the deceased's account in the name of the Probate Registrar to the applicants to enable them settle the Estate fee.

It is expected that you will act on this request promptly. An endorsed copy of this letter is forwarded to the applicants for their information, please.

........................., *ESQ*
PROBATE REGISTRAR

PED/…../20…./….
Probate Registry
High Court of Justice
Benin City.

…….20……….

Mr………………… & Anor.
…………………………………
…………………………………
Benin City.

Overleaf is for your information, reference letter dated …………… day of ………………., 20………..

………………………….. ESQ
PROBATE REGISTRAR

EDO STATE JUDICIARY
OFFICE OF THE PROBATE REGISTRAR
(PROBATE REGISTRY)
HIGH COURT OF JUSTICE
BENIN CITY

LETTER FOR MEAGRE SUM

OUR REF: PED/....../....... .... 2O......
YOUR REF:...................

The Manager,
.... Bank Plc.,
.... Branch
Benin City.

ESTATE OF .... DECEASED

Mr............................. and Mr ...., widower and Son respectively of the above –named deceased have applied to this office for a grant of Letters of Administration to administer the estate of the deceased.

An Inventory of the personal property of the deceased filed in this office by them shows that the deceased had a balance of N................. (amount in words) in her account with your Bank. This forms the only estate which the applicants seek to administer and as the amount is meagre, the financial involvement in procuring the Letters of Administration will outweigh the residue of the estate, thus rendering the Letters of Administration not worth their while.

It is in the light of the foregoing that I am requesting you to pay the said balance in the deceased's account No............ to Mr. .... and Mr ...., on the strength of their letter attached hereto.

We count on your co-operation, please.

......................, *ESQ*
PROBATE REGISTRAR

LETTER TO MINISTRY OF LANDS

EDO STATE JUDICIARY
OFFICE OF THE PROBATE REGISTRAR
(PROBATE REGISTRAR)
HIGH COURT OF JUSTICE
BENIN CITY

OUR REF: PED/....../......   ...... 20......
YOUR REF:..................

The Honourable Commissioner,
Ministry of Lands,
Benin City.

<u>ESTATE OF .... DECEASED</u>

I am directed to inform you that Mr............................... and Miss.......................... , Son and Daughter respectively of the above-named deceased have applied to this office for a grant of Letters of Administration to administer the estate of the deceased.

It will be appreciated if you make necessary arrangement for a valuation officer in your office to inspect and thereafter furnish this office with the value of the Real Properties mentioned below.

<u>REAL PROPERTIES</u>

1................................
2................................
3................................

Your early action will be appreciated, please.

For: PROBATE REGISTRAR

PED/…./………..
Probate Registry,
High court of Justice,
Benin City.
…… 20……..

Service on:
Mr. ……………………
…………………………
…………………………

Above is for your information, please. It will be appreciated if you call at the above mentioned address on any working day to act as pointers to the valuation officer that may be sent from the office, please.

……………………………
For: PROBATE REGISTRAR

OFFICE OF THE PROBATE REGISTRAR
(PROBATE REGISTRAR)
HIGH COURT OF JUSTICE
BENIN CITY

LETTER OF INVITATION TO ATTEND MEETING WITH THE PROBATE REGISTRAR EDO STATE JUDICIARY

OUR REF: PED/....../...... ....20......
YOUR REF:..................

Mrs.......................................
....
....

Mr...
....
....

Chief......................................
....
....

ESTATE OF ....DECEASED

I am directed to refer to the above-named deceased's estate and to request that you call at this office at 10. 00am prompt on Monday, the ...... day of ...., 20........., for an important discussion touching on the Administration of the deceased's estate.

Your co-operation will be highly appreciated, please.

....
For: PROBATE REGISTRAR

LETTER OF INVITATION FOR READING OF WILL

EDO STATE JUDICIARY
OFFICE OF THE PROBATE REGISTRAR
(PROBATE REGISTRY)
HIGH COURT OF JUSTICE
BENIN CITY

OUR REF: PED/……./…… ….. 20…….
YOUR REF:………………
…………………….., ESQ.,
……………………………,
……………………………,

RE: READING OF THE LAST WILL AND TESTAMENTOF CHIEF ………………..………DECEASED

I am directed to refer to your letter dated ……. day of ……., 20……. And to inform you that the Last Will of the above-named deceased will be opened and read to members of his family on Wednesday the ……… Day of…………, 20…… at 10.00am prompt.

It will be appreciated, if you make necessary arrangement for the Executors, Children and close Relations of the deceased to be present on the said date to witness the event, please.

……………………………...
For: PROBATE REGISTRAR

EXECUTORS:
Chief……………………,
…………………………..,
…………………………..,
Pastor……………………,
…………………………..,
……………………………,
Mr ……………………….,
……………………………..,
……………………………..,

LETTER TO REMIT ESTATE FEE

EDO STATE JUDICIARY
OFFICE OF THE PROBATE REGISTRAR
(PROBATE REGISTRY)
HIGH COURT OF JUSTICE
BENIN CITY

OUR REF: PED/....../...... ......, 20.......
YOUR REF:..................

.... ESQ.,
..................................,
....

RE: MR.. -DECEASED

I am directed to refer to your application dated the .... day of .... , 20......... For Probate in respect of the above-named deceased's estate and request you to remit to this office, the sum of N....................... (amount in words) only as estate fee, please.

....
For: PROBATE REGISTRAR

MINUTE

IN THE HIGH COURT OF JUSTICE, EDO STATE OF NIGERIA

BEFORE THE HONORABLE JUSTICE…………………. –CHIEF JUDGE

DATED THIS ………. DAY OF …………… 20………

PED/……../…………

IN CHAMBERS:-

IN THE MATTER OF GRANTING LETTERS OF ADMINISTRATION OF THE PERSONAL PROPERTY OF MRS. ………………..…………………… – DECEASED

UPON READING the application dated …. day of ………, 20…… of Mr…………………… and Miss………………., son and daughter respectively of the deceased for a grant of Letters of Administration of the personal property of the deceased and due advertisement having been made.

AND UPON FURTHER READING the Oath for Administration of the said MR. …………………….. and Miss……………………, sworn to on the …… day of ……….., 20……. the Administration Bond of MR. ………………….., MISS….……………………… Pastor………………… and Chief …………………, executed on the ……. Day of ……….., 20……. and the Justification of Sureties of Pastor…………………… and Chief……………………., sworn to on the …… day of ………………… , 20…………

IT IS HEREBY ORDERED that a grant of Letters of Administration of the personal property of the above-named deceased do pass under the seal of the High Court of Edo State of Nigeria to Mr. ………………… and Miss ……………….., son and daughter respectively of the deceased.

INVENTORY: ₦……………

BOND : ₦………………

CHIEF JUDGE

DATE…………………………………

MIUNTE (WITH RENUNCIATION)

IN THE HIGH COURT OF JUSTICE, EDO STATE OF NIGERIA

BEFORE THE HONOURABLE JUSTICE ....CHIEF JUDGE

DATED, THIS ...... DAY OF .... 20......

PED/........./.......

IN-CHAMBERS:-

IN THE MATTER OF GRANTING LETTERS OF ADMINISTRATION OF THE PERSONAL PROPERTY OF CHIEF...DECEASED

UPON READING the application dated .... day of ...., 20......of Mr. .... and Mr. ...., sons of the deceased for a grant of Letters of Administration of the personal property of the deceased and due advertisement having been made.

Upon reading the Renunciation of Mrs. .... and Mrs............., sworn to on the ...... Day of ...., 20......

AND UPON FURTHER READING the Oath for Administration of the said Mr.................... and Mr...................., sworn to on the ...... day of ...., 20....., the Administration Bond of Mr........................., Mr............................., Mrs....................... and Mr..............................., executed on the ...... day of ...., 20...... And the Justification of Sureties of Mrs............................. And Mr........................., sworn to on the ...... day of ...., 20............

IT IS HEREBY ORDERED that a grant of Letters of Administration of the personal property of the above-named deceased do pass under the seal of the High Court of Edo State of Nigeria to Mr…………………… and Mr………………, sons of the deceased.

INVENTORY : ₦……………

BOND : ₦……………

CHIEF JUDGE

DATE……………………

NOTICE OF APPLICATION TO PERSONS HAVING EQUAL RIGHT

OUR REF: PED/……./……..

IN THE HIGH COURT OF JUSTICE
EDO STATE OF NIGERIA

NOTICE OF APPLICATION FOR LETTERS OF ADMINISTRATION

IN THE ESTATE OF……………………….DECEASED

TAKE NOTICE the an application for grant of Letters of Administration in respect of the estate of the above-named deceased has been filed in the Probate Registry of the Court of Edo State by

____

____

____

________________________________of the deceased.

2. You should let me know within 14 days of service of this Notice on you whether you have any Objection to the grant being made to ____________________________________

____

____

DATED AT BENIN CITY, THIS ___ DAY OF _____ 20___

…………………………..

For: PROBATE REGISTRAR

NOTICE OF APPLICATION TO PERSONS HAVING PRIOR RIGHT

Probate Registry,
High Court of Justice,
Benin City.
…….. 20……….

OUR REF: PED/…./……

Dear Sir/Madam,

ESTATE OF……………………………… DECEASED

I am directed to inform you that an application for grant of Letters of Administration in respect of the real/personal property of the above-named deceased has been filed in this Registry by

……………………………………………………………………

……………………………………………………………………

……….. deceased.

2. In this connection I am inviting your attention to the fact that you have prior right of Administration over

……………………………………………………………………

……………………………………………………………………

You should therefore apply to this office if you wish to exercise your right.

3. If however you are unwilling to exercise your right you should renounce Administration by completing the attached renunciation form before a Commissioner for Oaths in the Magistrate's Court or High Court nearest to you to whom a swearing fee……….. is payable. Therefore you should call at this office bringing along with the renunciation form and a filing fee of ………..

4. I have to add that Renunciation of Administration does not disinherit you of your share of the deceased's estate but only precludes you from the Administration.

Yours Faithfully

For: PROBATE REGISTRAR

IN THE HIGH COURT OF JUSTICE
EDO STATE OF NIGERIA

OATH FOR ADMINISTRATOR (WILL ANNEXED)

IN THE MATTER OF .... DECEASED
I.. of .... make Oath and say that I believe the paper writing ....hereto annexed and marked by me, to contain the true and original Last Will of .... late of .... deceased; that ....
....
that I am the .... named therein, that I will faithfully administer the personal property of the Testator by paying his just debts and the legacies given by his Will... so far as his personal property shall extend and the law bind me, and distributing the residue of his personal property according to law : that I will exhibit an Inventory and render an account of my administration whenever lawfully required, that the Testator died at .... on the....... day of............. 20...... that at the time of his death he had his fixed place of abode at .... within the jurisdiction of this Court : and that the whole of his personal property does not amount in value to the sum of ...., Naira, to the best of my knowledge, information and belief.

Sworn to at......... this......... day of .... 20....

BEFORE ME: 1 ....
2 ....
3 ....
4 ....

....

COMMISSIONER FOR OATHS

IN THE HIGH COURT OF JUSTICE
EDO STATE OF NIGERIA

OATH FOR ADMINISTRATION (WITHOUT WILL)

IN THE MATTER OF.............................. DECEASED
of...
we..make Oath and say, that .... late of .... deceased, died Intestate of .... and that we are...

That we will faithfully administer the personal and real property of the deceased, by paying ...., just debts and distributing the residue of.........Personal property according to law.

That we will exhibit an Inventory and render an account of our administration as lawfully required.

That the deceased died at............ on the.....day of ...... 20......

That at the time of .... death .... had .... fixed place of abode at .... within the jurisdiction of this Court.

And that the whole of .... personal and real property does not exceed in value the sum of .... Naira to the best of our knowledge, information and belief.

SWORN TO AT ...... THIS .... DAY OF ...... 20.......

	1.	....
	2.	....
Signature of Applicants	3.	....
	4.	....

BEFORE ME

COMMISSIONER FOR OATHS

IN THE HIGH COURT OF JUSTICE
EDO STATE OF NIGERIA

OATH FOR EXECUTOR

IN THE MATTER OF.............................. DECEASED

I, ... of ....
.... make Oath and say: that .... I believe the paper writing hereto annexed and marked by .... to contain the true and original Last Will of .... late of .... deceased, and that ....
The Executor therein named, and that .... will faithfully administer the personal property of the Testat .... by paying .... just debts and the legacies given by .... Will so far as .... personal property shall extend and the law bind .... that ....will exhibit an Inventory and render an account of .... Executorship as lawfully required. That the Testat .... died at .... on the ...... day of .... 20...... and that at the time of ...., death .... had .... fixed place of abode at .... within the jurisdiction of this Court, and that the whole of .... personal property does not amount in value to the sum of .... Naira to the best of .... Knowledge, information and belief.

SWORN TO AT .... THIS...... DAY OF .... 20......

BEFORE ME

COMMISSIONER FOR OATHS

ORDER

PED/....../.........
Probate Registry,
High Court of Justice,
Benin City.

The Honourable,
The Chief Judge,
High Court of Justice
Benin City.
My Lord,

CHIEF...DECEASED

Papers herein are submitted with the Order Book.

2. (a) Inventory of the personal property of the above-named deceased has been taken and valued at N ....
   (b) Notices of application have been posted and advertisement inserted in the Observer Newspaper of .... Day of ...., 20 ......
   (c) Bond in the sum of N........................... executed
   (d) All fees have been paid and
   (e) NO CAVEAT LODGED
3. May Letters of Administration of the personal property of the above-named Deceased issue to the petitioners:-

MR................................

AND

MR.................................

(SONS OF THE DECEASED)

DATED THIS......... DAY OF ...., 20.......

......................., *ESQ*

PROBATE REGISTRAR

ORDER AS PRAYED
CHIEF JUDGE

DATE...........................

IN THE HIGH COURT OF JUSTICE
EDO STATE 0F NIGERIA

LETTERS OF ADMINISTRATION
(WILL ANNEXED)
PROBATE

IN THE MATTER OF .... DECEASED

BE IT KNOWN THAT ON THE.... Day of .... 20... the Last Will .... (a copy whereof is hereto annexed) late of .... deceased, who died on the .... day of .... 20...... at .... And who at the time of .... death had .... fixed place of abode at .... within the jurisdiction of this Court, was proved and registered in this Court, and that the Administration of the real and personal property of the said deceased was granted by this Court to .... the .... Execut .... named in the said Will .... having been first duly sworn.

Sworn under N.............. and that the Testat .... died on or about the ...... Day of .... 20 ......

.... *ESQ*
PROBATE REGISTRAR

Seal of Court

SCHEDULE OF FEES

File and Tag .... N
Application for Letters of Administration .... N
Swearing persons to inventory .... N
Filing inventory form .... N
Swearing persons to Declaration as to Next-of- Kin form ...N
Filing Declaration as to Next-of-Kin form .... N
Legal Notice Publication .... N
Oath in Oath for Administration form .... N
Filing Oath for Administration form .... N
Attestation signatures on Bond .... N
Filing Administration Bond form .... N
Drawing up of Administration Decree .... N
Oath in and filing renunciation form ..... N
Oath in and filing Justification of Sureties form ...... N
Estate fees ...... N

____

____

RECEIPTS LISTED

PR/ CR NO. .... of ...../...../2019 .... N
PR/ CR NO. .... of ...../...../2019 .... N
PR/ CR NO. .... of ...../...../2019 .... N
PR/CR NO. .... of ...../...../2019 .... N

____

____

IN THE HIGH COURT OFJUSTICE
EDO STATE OF NIGERIA
PROBATE REGISTRY

RENUNCIATION OF ADMINISTRATION (WITHOUT WILL)

IN THE MATTER OF ………………………… DECEASED WHEREAS ……………………….. late of …………………… Deceased, died on the ……………………… Day of ……….. 20…… at……………………………………… intestate, having had at the time of …………………………… death ………………………… fixed place of abode at ……………………… within the jurisdiction of this Court.

And whereas I, ……………………………………… of …………………………………………………………………

Now, I, the said ………………………………………..... do hereby declare that I have not intermeddled in the personal property of the deceased, and further do hereby expressly renounce all right to the Administration thereof.

In witness whereof I have hereto set my hand this …… day of ………….. 20 ……

Signed by the said ________________

………………………………

In the presence of

COMMISSIONER FOR OATHS

IN THE HIGH COURT OF JUSTICE
EDO STATE OF NIGERIA
PROBATE REGISTRY

RENUNCIATION OF PROBATE

IN THE MATTER OF .... DECEASED
WHEREAS .... late of .... deceased, died on the ..... day of .... 20...... at .... having made and duly executed his Last Will and Testament, bearing date the ...... day of ...., 20......, and thereof appointed .... the undersigned .... his Executor(s)

Now I, the said .... do hereby declare that I have not intermeddled in the estate of the said deceased, and will not hereafter intermeddled therein with the intent to defraud Creditors, and I do hereby renounce all my right and title to Probate and execution of the said Will of the estate of the said deceased.

In witness whereof I have hereto set my hand this.........day of.............., 20.............

Signed by the said ________________

In the presence of

....

COMMISSIONER FOR OATHS

IN THE HIGH COURT OF JUSTICE
EDO STATE OF NIGERIA
PROBATE REGISTRY

RESEALING CERTIFICATE

IN THE MATTER OF THE ESTATE OF ………DECEASED RE-SEALED by the direction of the High Court of Edo State of Nigeria, this ……… day of …………., 20 ……..
Estate sworn under N …………………… And the deceased died on ……….. day of………………., 20………

Assets Declared:

Personal Property

Real Property

DATED this……….. day of ……………., 20………

……………………….., ***ESQ***
PROBATE REGISTRAR

FORM 54

(O. 59, r. 57 (2), (7)
WARNING OF CAVEATOR
IN THE HIGH COURT OF EDO STATE
PROBATE REGISTRY

SUIT NO...............

To .... of .... a party who has entered a caveat in the estate of .... Deceased, you are hereby warned within eight days after service hereof upon you, inclusive of the day of such service:

1. To enter an appearance either in person or by your legal practitioner, at the Probate Registry, setting forth what interest you have in the estate of the above-named deceased, contrary to that of the party at whose instance this warning is issued: or
2. If you have no contrary interest but wish to show cause against the sealing of a grant to such party, to issue and serve a summons for direction by the registrar of the said Registry.

And take notice that in default of your so doing, the Court may proceed to issue a grant of probate or administration in the said estate not withstanding your caveat.

DATED this ...... day of ...., 20......

....

Registrar

Issued at the instance of (here set out the name and interest, including the date of the Will if any, under which the interest arises) the party warning, the name of his legal practitioner and the address for service, (if the party warning is acting in person, this must be stated)

PROBATE AND ADMINISTRATION OF ESTATE (FEES PAYABLE)

(1) On filing an application for Probate or Letters of Administration N200.00
(2) On filing Oath of Executor or Administration N200.00
(3) On taking justification of sureties for each survey N100.00
(4) On filing Administration Bond.................................... N100.00
(5) On entering a Caveat N500.00
(6) On every warning to a Caveat N200.00
(7) On application for Probate or Letters of or order for Administration: 10% of the total value of the property which exceeds .... N50,000.00 (Provided that the 10% Probate fee in respect of pensioners Entitlement would be deducted at the point of payment).
(8) Deposit of Will for safe custody N2,000.00
(9) Sealing and Certification of Will N500.00
(10) Sealing and Certification of Codicil N500.00
(11) Filing of Debts and Funeral N500.00
(12) Drawing up of Order or Grant N200.00
(13) Swearing and filing of Affidavit of Alias N500.00
(14) Application to search index to Grant or Wills N500.00
(15) Inspection of Grants or Wills N500.00

BIBLIOGRAPHY

RULES OF COURT

Delta State High Court (Civil Procedure) Rules, 2009

Edo State High Court (Civil Procedure) Rules, 2018

Lagos State High Court (Civil Procedure) Rules, 2012

STATUTE

Administration Of Estate Law, Cap.2 Vol. I Laws Of Defunct Bendel State Of Nigeria1976 As Applicable In Edo State.

Wills Laws, Cap.172 Vol.VI Laws Of Defunct Bendel State Of Nigeria 1976 As Applicable In Edo State.

BOOKS

Abayomi, Kole "Wills: Law And Practice", Mbeyi & Associates (Nig.) Ltd, 2004.

Momodu, B. "Encyclopedia of Nigeria Case Law Principles And Authorities", Momodu B. Law Publishing, Benin City, 2018.

Mosanya, J. A., "Common Form Probate Business", Mbeyi & Associates (Nig.) Ltd., Lagos, 2007

Imhanobe, S. O., "Legal Drafting And Conveyancing", (2nd Edition) Sylvester Imhanobe Legal Research Ltd, Abuja, 2007.

SEMINAR PAPER

Otoghile, J. O.,: The Place Of A Will In Relation To Igiogbe Inheritance", A Seminar Paper Presented As A Ph. D Student In The Faculty Of Law, Ambrose Alli University, Ekpoma, Edo State, Nigeria, (2016).